The Hidden Power of
THE BLOOD
of JESUS

The Hidden Power of
THE BLOOD
of JESUS

MAHESH CHAVDA

Destiny Image® Publishers, Inc.
P.O. Box 310
Shippensburg, PA 17257-0310

"Speaking to the Purposes of God for This Generation
and for the Generations to Come"

ISBN 0-7684-2222-1

For Worldwide Distribution
Printed in the U.S.A.

3 4 5 6 7 8 9 10 11 12 13 14 15 / 10 09 08 07 06 05 04

This book and all other Destiny Image, Revival Press, MercyPlace, Fresh Bread, Destiny Image Fiction, and Treasure House books are available at Christian bookstores and distributors worldwide.

For a U.S. bookstore nearest you, call
1-800-722-6774.
For more information on foreign distributors, call
717-532-3040.
Or reach us on the Internet:
www.destinyimage.com

Contents

Chapter One

ONE DROP OF BLOOD

Some years ago I traveled to central Africa, to Kinshasa, the capital city of Zaire. Upon arrival, I found myself in the middle of a mighty visitation of God. It was none of my doing. I had left home in the midst of a tremendous family crisis. Bonnie, my wife, had just delivered a son prematurely after a difficult and troubled pregnancy. At birth, Aaron weighed only one and a half pounds, and soon after, dropped to one pound, three ounces. The doctors offered little hope for his survival.

I had a long-standing commitment to proclaim the gospel in Zaire, but with Aaron's life hanging in the balance, I was torn. Bonnie said to me, "Honey, your place is out there. God will take care of us." After anointing Aaron with oil, I committed him and Bonnie to the Lord's care, and departed for Africa. It looked as though I would never see my precious son again.[1]

Because I was so preoccupied with matters at home, I never expected the major revival that visited Zaire as a result of my evangelistic meetings. Hundreds of miracles occurred

---

1. God miraculously healed Aaron while I was in Zaire, and today he is a robust and healthy young man. Isn't God great!

every night. Never in my wildest imagination had I dreamed that I would ever see with my own eyes some of the marvelous things I witnessed that week.

People bound in chains just like the Gadarene demoniac (see Mark 5:1-17) were running around crying, struggling, and trying to attack those around them. Then, as the power of God hit them, they fell to the ground and got up completely delivered of their demons. I saw eyesight given to people who were born blind. Night after night I saw miracle after miracle as thousands of Africans came forward and placed their faith in the Lord Jesus Christ.

The crowds grew in size every night until, by Friday, attendance exceeded 130,000. That night, the local pastors who had been working with me said, "Brother Mahesh, this is a week night; the main crowds will come on the weekend."

I said, "What do you mean the 'main crowds'? I'm happy with this one!"

Confronting the Sorcerers

When I got up the next day, I heard the Lord say to me, "Tonight you will do a mass deliverance service."

"But Lord," I protested, "tonight is when the biggest crowd will be coming!" I still remembered the time when Brother Derek Prince and I had held a mass deliverance service for 10,000 people. In that part of Africa, strongholds of witchcraft were so powerful that when we took authority in the name of Jesus, a couple hundred people fell down and started writhing like snakes and coming toward us. God miraculously delivered them. Now, years later, here I was with a crowd more than ten times larger.

The Lord told me again, "Tonight you will do a mass deliverance service."

"Lord," I replied, "if I do that, thousands of demons will manifest and we will be out of control!" I was all alone, with no trained staff to help me. A few local pastors were assisting me, but they were not trained in deliverance ministry.

I asked, "How can You do this, Lord? I'm all alone."

He answered, "Tonight, hundreds of sorcerers will come and confront you."

This wasn't getting any better. I felt like saying, "Thanks a lot! I wish You had never told me!"

You have to understand that these African sorcerers are not the type who just play with Ouija boards or give astrological signs to people. They are the kind of sorcerers who place curses on people, and those people actually die. According to some, these sorcerers can supposedly change forms at night, and they are known to eat human flesh regularly. Far beyond your "garden-variety" sorcerer, these necromancers are completely devoted to the forces of evil and darkness. Because they have given themselves over to satan, they possess demonic powers.

And now *hundreds* of them were going to confront me? Again I tried to reason with God. "Lord, I'm all alone here, and You really want me to hold a deliverance service to cast demons out of *thousands* of people?"

The Lord said, "This night I am sending you to break the yoke of witchcraft over this nation."

"But Lord," I pleaded, "I'm all alone!"

What I heard next sealed it for me. God really spoke to my heart. His presence was so close that I heard Him almost as an audible voice. "You are not alone, for I am your helper. *Tonight I will give you a revelation of My blood.*"

That evening, approximately 800 sorcerers from all over that region of Africa were among the tens of thousands gathered in that place. *One* sorcerer alone was enough to strike fear into an entire village. Over the past several days, these shamans had seen thousands of people come to Christ. Now, angry because I had taken business away from them, they had come together to oppose my ministry. Although scattered throughout the crowd, they were easy enough to identify. Their bone necklaces and strange manner of dress set them apart from everybody else.

The local African pastors came to me in fear and said, "These sorcerers are putting their curses upon us and upon the service! What should we do?"

"Let them do it," I replied.

It is very difficult to describe, but as I began that night, I realized that I had walked into a highly-charged spiritual atmosphere. It was almost as though I could see the blood of Jesus Christ all around me. As I stood up to speak, something exploded inside me, and I said, "I know you are out there, all you sorcerers, and I want you to know that I am not afraid of you. Not one person here tonight needs to be afraid of the powers of darkness. Listen to me, sorcerers. I am not afraid of you, and I am not afraid of your demons. Tonight, God has shown me that *one drop of the blood of Jesus Christ can destroy the kingdom of satan*!"

Mass Deliverance

As the Lord had promised, it was a true revelation for me. That night we bound the powers of darkness, and God brought a mighty deliverance. I said, "In the name of Jesus, I bind you demon spirits who have oppressed this people for centuries. I break that yoke of witchcraft; I release this people."

Even as I prayed, thousands of demons began manifesting. People fell to the ground. Sick bodies were healed, and blind eyes were opened. Many people who were involved in witchcraft renounced their sorcery. In addition to the miraculous physical healings, masses of people were transformed spiritually by the power of the blood of Jesus. The sorcerers' powers were bound. At one point, the local pastors rushed up to me excitedly and said, "Brother Mahesh, we believe that as many as 25,000 people have given their lives to Jesus Christ tonight!"

Here is the amazing thing. I had done deliverance services before, and it was very common for demons to wail out and cause quite a commotion when we commanded them to leave. On this occasion, I was looking out over a crowd of around 150,000 people, and I was afraid of things getting really strange and out of control. After a little while, when I sensed that the Holy Spirit had done what He was going to do, I said, "In the power of the name of Jesus and through His blood, I command you to stop." The entire place became absolutely quiet. I had never seen anything like it: 150,000 people gathered in one place, and complete silence.

The Lord taught me two lessons that night: there is power in the blood of Jesus Christ, and every demon has to bow when we walk in the revelation of that blood.

We Need the Revelation of the Blood

Africa is not unique. All over the world, in every nation, culture, and people group, millions of people stand in need of a deliverance that only the blood of Jesus Christ can bring. Even within the Body of Christ itself—the church—many believers are in spiritual bondage through sin and ignorance and need deliverance. In many cases, they have never been taught the power of the blood of Jesus to bring them the healing they need. Our Lord's purpose is for us, His people, to bring salvation, healing, and deliverance to the nations. How can we do that if we need to be delivered ourselves?

Our world has entered a very special and prophetic time in history. God is always at work, but what is He doing right now? How do we catch the pulse of God's heart for today? In order to get a sense of what God is doing in His people, the church, we need to see what He is doing in the Jews and the nation of Israel.

At the same time that God established the modern nation of Israel in 1948, He also released a season of powerful and significant evangelistic and healing ministries unparalleled in history. Churches grew up by the thousands as people like Billy Graham, T. L. Osborn, William Brenham, Gordon Lindsey, Oral Roberts, Kathryn Kuhlman, and others boldly proclaimed the gospel of Jesus Christ with power on a national and international scale never before seen.

In recent years we have witnessed a mass exodus of Jews from around the globe—but especially Russia—to Israel. Not since the biblical exodus of Moses' day has the world seen such a migration of God's covenant people back to their homeland. In many cases, as with Russia, they were fleeing persecution. As it was in ancient times, anti-Semitism is alive and well in our world. Even as hatred and anti-Jewish prejudice are on the rise, God is delivering His covenant people and bringing them home in increasing numbers.

Today we are eyewitnesses to the fulfillment of the Lord's promise in Jeremiah and Ezekiel:

> *In those days the house of Judah shall walk with the house of Israel, and they shall come together out of the land of the north to the land that I have given for an inheritance unto your fathers* (Jeremiah 3:18).

> *Therefore say, Thus saith the Lord God; Although I have cast them far off among the heathen, and although I have scattered them among the countries, yet will I be to them as a little sanctuary in the countries where they shall come. Therefore say, Thus saith the Lord God; I will gather you from the people, and assemble you out of the countries where ye have been scattered, and I will give you the land of Israel* (Ezekiel 11:16-17).

God is fulfilling His Word before our very eyes. No matter how powerful the forces of evil and darkness appear, God is in charge of history. He always has been.

In this present generation, the Lord wants to impregnate us with a deep sense of who we are as His people. This is not a time to circle the wagons; we should be in "attack mode." This is the hour where we should run toward the enemy, pull down his strongholds, and take back the nations. One drop of the blood of Jesus is all it takes to destroy satan's kingdom, and God wants us to receive His revelation of that blood.

He calls each of us to stand as points of contact not only for ourselves, but also for all we represent: our family members, especially those who are unsaved, our schools, and our businesses and places of employment. The Lord wants us to stand in His anointing and in this revelation of the blood of

Jesus Christ. He wants us to walk in it and take it with us wherever we go.

Delivered by the Blood

The ancient nation of Israel had a revelation of the blood of Jesus, and it brought them deliverance. As descendants of Abraham, who had received God's promise that he would be the father of a great nation, the Israelites were God's chosen people. They were heirs to all the promises God had given Abraham. Nevertheless, in spite of those promises, they spent 450 years as slaves in Egypt before the Lord sent Moses to deliver them.

By the time Moses arrived on the scene, life for the Israelites was in a deplorable state. During their long, hard years of slavery, the Israelites could hardly avoid being influenced by the false religion of the Egyptians. Many Israelites had gone so far as to begin worshiping the gods of Egypt. The brutal, grueling nature of their slave labor undoubtedly resulted in many crippling injuries such as loss of an eye; crushed fingers, toes, or limbs; and amputations. They were malnourished, suffered continually under cruel Egyptian taskmasters, and lived in abject poverty with very little they could call their own. As slaves, they did not even own themselves.

Then the Lord stepped in and said, "I'm going to deliver you." Through Moses, God instructed the people to slaughter a lamb on the 14th day of the month and spread its blood on the lintels and doorposts of their houses. Why did God give such a strange command? What did it mean? The Lord was about to let loose the destroyer in the land of Egypt, and He wanted His people to be protected:

*For I will pass through the land of Egypt this night,
and will smite all the firstborn in the land of Egypt,
both man and beast; and against all the gods of
Egypt I will execute judgment: I am the LORD. And
the blood shall be to you a token upon the houses
where ye are: and when I see the blood, I will pass
over you, and the plague shall not be upon you to
destroy you, when I smite the land of Egypt* (Exodus
12:12-13).

That night, every firstborn in Egypt died, whether of man
or beast. It was different with the Israelites. Whenever the
destroyer saw the lamb's blood on the doorposts and lintels of
an Israelite home, he passed over that house and did not bring
death or harm to anyone inside.

Deliverance came swiftly. Even before that terrible night
was over, Pharaoh summoned Moses and told him to take the
Israelites and leave Egypt. Overnight, as many as four million
people were set free. They did not leave empty-handed. God
gave the Israelites favor in the eyes of the Egyptian people,
who showered them with articles of gold and silver, as well as
fine clothing. In this way, the Israelites "plundered" the Egyptians (see Exodus 12:36).

Through the blood, the Israelites received not only deliverance, but also healing. What about all the crippled and disease-wracked people among the Israelites? How could they
possibly hope to keep up during a hasty departure?

They did not have to. God healed them. Psalm 105:37
says, "He brought them forth with silver and gold: and there
was not one feeble person among their tribes." When God delivered His people from slavery in Egypt, He delivered them completely. Not only did He bring them out of the pagan

environment so they could worship Him exclusively, He also healed their infirmities so they could serve Him with whole, healthy bodies.

In one night, the Israelites experienced instant redemption from slavery. Because of the Passover blood, they were totally delivered from the oppressions of Egypt. The blood of the lamb that the Israelites smeared on their doorposts was a type and a shadow of the blood of the Lamb, Jesus Christ, who would later die on a cross to take away the sin of the world. By smearing the blood around their doors, they were looking ahead in faith to the blood of the Savior, the Lord Jesus Christ.

Israel left Egypt as a new and blessed nation, with abundant provision and wealth. A short time later in the wilderness of Sinai, they constructed the tabernacle and established the priesthood and the rituals for their worship. One of these rituals was the regular offering of blood for the sins of the people. Animal sacrifices were offered up daily, but every year on the Day of Atonement, the high priest entered the tabernacle and passed into the Holy of Holies, where the ark of the covenant was kept. There he made a special offering, sprinkling the blood of the lamb on the mercy seat to atone for the people's sins.

Leviticus chapter 16:14 says that the high priest sprinkled the blood seven times when making atonement for the people. Atonement means the "reconciliation of or restoration of fellowship." The blood of the sacrifice symbolically removed the barrier that sin had erected between God and His people. Through atonement, God could bless them, protect them, and keep them in good health, so that none of the diseases of Egypt would fall on them.

The people of Israel had to offer sacrifices over and over because the blood of an innocent animal could not take away their sin. Over the centuries, millions of lambs, goats, and rams were sacrificed as blood, guilt, and atonement offerings. All of these were only a foreshadowing of the sacrifice to come years later when Jesus gave His life on the cross.

As long as the Israelites obeyed God's covenant, they were a blessed people who walked in total victory. Even so, they had merely the shadow, while we have the reality. The shadow was the blood of animals, while the reality is the blood of Jesus that takes away the sin of the world. When the high priest on the Day of Atonement sprinkled the lamb's blood seven times on the mercy seat, he was looking ahead to the seven-fold offering of the blood of Jesus Christ.

Seven Ways Jesus Gave His Blood

The gospel of Jesus Christ is a message of *blood*; the blood of the Lamb of God slain from the foundation of the world. Satan and his demons hate this message about the blood of Jesus because it means their destruction. They quake at the very mention of Jesus' blood. Humanists and legalistic religionists also hate the message of the blood. To them, the idea that right-standing with God comes through Jesus' blood rather than by human effort is foolish and distasteful.

Nevertheless, there is no other way. Hebrews 9:22 says, "And almost all things are by the law purged with blood; and without shedding of blood there is no remission." In the words of the an old gospel hymn, "What can wash away my sin? Nothing but the blood of Jesus. What can make me whole again? Nothing but the blood of Jesus."

In studying the Scriptures, we find that the Bible mentions seven different ways that Jesus spilled His blood as He offered up His life as a sin sacrifice on our behalf:

1. *He sweated drops of blood.* "And being in agony He prayed more earnestly: and His sweat was as it were great drops of blood falling down to the ground" (Luke 22:44).

2. *He bled from beatings to His face.* "And when they had blindfolded Him, they struck Him on the face, and asked Him, saying, Prophesy, who is it that smote Thee?" (Luke 22:64) A Spanish translation gives the idea that Jesus' face was almost like hamburger meat.

3. *He bled from having His beard ripped out.* "I gave My back to those who struck Me, and My cheeks to those who plucked out the beard; I did not hide My face from shame and spitting" (Isaiah 50:6).

4. *He bled from a brutal scourging.* "Then he released Barabbas unto them: and when he had scourged Jesus, he delivered Him to be crucified" (Matthew 27:26). Jesus was flogged across His back, His sides, and even His abdomen with a multi-tipped whip with sharp pieces of metal and bone interlaced in the tips. A flogging with this device laid flesh open to the bone.

5. *He bled from a crown of thorns crushed onto His head.* "And when they had platted a crown of thorns, they put it upon His head" (Matthew 27:29a).

6. *He bled from nails driven through His hands and feet.* "And when they were come to the place, which is called Calvary, there they crucified Him" (Luke 23:33a).

7. *He bled from a Roman spear piercing His side.* "But one of the soldiers with a spear pierced His side, and forthwith came there out blood and water" (John 19:34).

One of the most glorious and powerful statements in the New Testament is found in John 1:29 where John the Baptist says of Jesus, "Behold the Lamb of God, which taketh away the sin of the world." It is such a simple, yet deeply profound, truth. What it means is that anyone in the world who will, can say, "Lord Jesus, please save me," and His blood will cleanse them of their sin.

I believe there is significance in the fact that Jesus shed His blood seven ways. In the Bible, numbers often represent qualities or conditions. The number seven stands for perfection or completeness, the sense of being full or satisfied. From that perspective, the seven-fold way that Jesus spilled His blood means that His was the perfect and complete sacrifice for sin that fully satisfies God's holy wrath.

There are many instances of "seven" in the Bible. God gave Abraham a seven-fold blessing:

And I will make of thee a great nation, and I will
bless thee, and make thy name great; and thou shalt
be a blessing: And I will bless them that bless thee,
and curse him that curseth thee: and in thee shall
all families of the earth be blessed (Genesis 12:2-3).

How did God fulfill His seven-fold blessing to Abraham? Through the seven-fold shedding of the blood of Christ, His Son.

God created all things in six days and rested on the seventh day. The Book of Revelation speaks of the "seven Spirits of God." In the Word of God, seven always stands for perfection. Ultimately, I believe, God is pointing us to the perfection of the seven-fold shedding of Jesus' blood. His blood makes us whole and complete. Nothing else is needed for our provision, our healing, or our welfare. The blood of Jesus has done it all. His blood covers us.

Overcoming Through the Blood

I am convinced that one of the major reasons so many of us live defeated lives as Christians is because we have never learned to apply the blood of Jesus to our circumstances to bring healing and wholeness. The blood of Christ has the ability to speak and intercede on our behalf before the Father, but so often we do not take advantage of that benefit, either out of ignorance or unbelief.

Hebrews 12:24 refers to "Jesus the Mediator of the new covenant, and to the blood of sprinkling, that speaketh better things than that of Abel." Jesus mediated the new covenant with His blood. According to Genesis 4:10, the voice of Abel's blood cried out to God, exposing Cain's sin of murder. Jesus' blood speaks even better than Abel's. The blood of Jesus speaks on our behalf, covering our sin and declaring us righteous—in right standing—before God.

Whenever I speak to congregations or audiences of any size, I rarely have to shout because I have the benefit of a good electronic sound system. In some parts of Africa, we rented giant public address systems where I could whisper and still be heard by 100,000 people or more. My voice was amplified. In the same way, when we pray and call on the name of the Lord—when we say "the blood of Jesus"—our prayers are amplified millions and millions of times, until the demons tremble. There is power in the blood of Jesus—power to move heaven and earth on our behalf in fulfillment of God's purposes.

Through the blood of Jesus we are a redeemed people. This means that Jesus bought us for salvation with His blood. Through the blood of Jesus we are a justified people. "Justified" is a legal term that means we have been declared "not guilty." Jesus took our sin and guilt so that we could be pardoned, just as if we had never sinned. Through the blood of Jesus we are a sanctified people. In other words, now that we are redeemed and justified, we are set apart as God's special people to love Him, live for Him, and bring Him glory.

Through the blood of Jesus we have access to the holy presence of God. Hebrews 10:19 says that we can have "boldness to enter the holiest by the blood of Jesus." Access to the presence of God means that all of His resources and provisions are available to us. Without the blood of Jesus, we have no access. We are powerless, destitute, and separated from God because of our sins. The blood of Jesus covers our sin, clothes us in Christ's righteousness, and brings us into close fellowship with the Father. In His presence we find grace, peace, and the power to overcome the enemy.

Neither satan nor any of his demonic minions can stand against the power of the blood of Jesus. When we are covered by His blood, the enemy cannot hurt us.

> *And I heard a loud voice saying in heaven, Now is come salvation, and strength, and the kingdom of our God, and the power of His Christ: for the accuser of our brethren is cast down, which accused them before our God day and night. And they overcame him by the blood of the Lamb, and by the word of their testimony; and they loved not their lives unto the death"* (Revelation 12:10-11).

Satan is the "accuser of our brethren" who "is cast down." "They" in verse 11 refers to "our brethren," meaning all who have trusted in Christ as Lord and Savior. That includes you and me. We have overcome our accuser by "the blood of the Lamb," and by "the word of [our] testimony."

Jesus is the Lamb of God who takes away the sin of the world. When we stand covered by the blood of Jesus, the devil has no grounds for accusing us anymore. When he tries to throw our sinfulness and failures in our faces, we can testify, "The blood of Jesus covers me and has washed away my sins. I now stand clothed in His righteousness, clean and pure before God, just as if I had never sinned."

Our sin is the only basis satan has for accusing us. Once our sin is removed by the blood of Jesus, the devil loses any hold he had on our lives. The only power satan has over us as believers is the power we allow him to have. Sin, disobedience, rebellion, and unbelief on our part open the door that allows the devil to get a foothold in our hearts and minds. We can overcome him by the blood of Jesus, but we must be walking in faith and obedience.

As Christians, we are destined to overcome. Victory is the only *outcome* because we *overcome* with the blood of Jesus Christ. By faith, we sprinkle His blood that overcomes, and the demons tremble. Because of the blood of Christ, we can overcome adultery, homosexuality, spiritual darkness, disease, divorce, drug addiction, alcohol addiction—anything that tempts us or threatens to destroy our lives or the lives of those we love. We can overcome all things through the blood of Jesus. One drop of His blood can destroy satan's kingdom.

Delivered from the Oppression of Perversion

In 1973 I was a young pastor in Texas just beginning to get a good handle on the truths about principalities, powers, the reality of demons, and the power of the blood of Jesus. One day the phone rang. Two Pentecostal pastors were on the line. "Brother Mahesh," they began, "we're in trouble."

"What's the problem?"

"We were counseling a young man who is a homosexual, when suddenly he spoke to us in a very strange voice, saying that he wanted to have fellowship with us. We can sense the evil here, and we are afraid."

"You are men of God," I replied. "What are you afraid of?"

They simply said, "Please, Brother Mahesh, we need your help."

"All right; I will come over."

When I arrived at their church, I found them hiding in one of the rooms. "What are you doing in here?" I asked.

"We are afraid because the demons were speaking to us."

"Well," I said, "speak back! Talk to them!"

They said, "Please, will you do it?"

The moment I entered the room where the young man was, I could feel the powers of darkness there. A demon had manifested in this man, and it was a strong one. I found out that the man had been a homosexual for about 18 years. All that time something inside had driven him with a sexual hunger for other men. As soon as I looked at this young man, I saw something looking back at me, something in his eyes that was not him. A different personality was present, an evil and demonic personality.

He said to me, "They asked you to come. I know they did. Come on, I want to have fellowship with you." The man had been around Christians enough to know some of the terms, such as "fellowship," but was using them in evil and distorted ways. It was actually the demon speaking to me.

"All right," I replied. "If you want to fellowship with me, that's fine. The Bible says, 'If we walk in the light as He is in the light, we have fellowship with one another, and the blood of Jesus Christ His Son cleanses us from all sin.' Do you want to fellowship with me? Then say, 'the blood of Jesus.' Come on, say it right now."

The man started moaning and writhing, and his fingers, hands, and ankles started twisting and contorting unnaturally. I could actually hear his joints and knuckles crackling.

"Stop that!" I said. "I don't want that demonstration right now. Say, " 'the blood of Jesus.' "

He babbled incoherently for a few moments, and then suddenly the demon departed, screaming. It could not stand up to the power of the blood of Jesus. Even the *mention* of the blood was enough to send it packing.

A few years later, I returned to Texas, and this same man made an appointment to see me. He said, "Brother Mahesh, do you remember that I was a homosexual for 18 years?"

"Yes."

"Well, I have a surprise for you." He then introduced me to a beautiful young woman. Smiling, he said, "This is my lovely wife, and we have been married for five years. When you prayed for me that day, that demon of homosexuality left me, and I have been clean ever since. I was totally delivered."

This man was delivered by the power of the blood of Jesus. One drop of Jesus' blood can destroy the kingdom of satan. None of his works or schemes can stand against the blood of the Lamb of God. His blood works on our behalf. Through His blood we are delivered and protected from all the schemes of the enemy. With the blood of Jesus, we are a victorious army of God, marching to tear down the strongholds of the enemy: addiction, homosexuality, pornography, lust, fear, pride, hatred, prejudice, or whatever else they might be. We can overcome them all through the blood of the Lamb and the word of our testimony. One drop of Jesus' blood is all it takes.

Chapter Two

PASSOVER BLOOD

Two thousand years ago the Son of God came to earth to redeem the sons of men. Jesus Christ died a criminal's death to buy our freedom from the bondage of sin. He purchased our release at the price of His own blood.

Without the blood of Jesus we have no hope. Without the blood of Jesus we have no purpose or direction for our lives. Just look around. Everywhere we turn people are stumbling aimlessly and hopelessly through life, full of despair and overwhelmed with a deep sense of futility. These folks have never discovered the power of the blood of Jesus to cleanse their sin and give their lives meaning and purpose.

Nothing less than the blood of Jesus will suffice. The Bible says that sin has corrupted the entire human race, beginning with Adam and Eve. Only something incorruptible can redeem the corruptible. Only that which is untainted by sin can redeem the sinful. No treasure on earth can fill the bill. Our redemption can come only from heaven.

This is the point Peter was trying to make when he wrote:

And if ye call on the Father, who without respect of persons judgeth according to every man's work,

pass the time of your sojourning here in fear: Foras-
much as ye know that ye were not redeemed with
corruptible things, as silver and gold, from your vain
conversation received by tradition from your fathers;
But with the precious blood of Christ, as of a lamb
without blemish and without spot (1 Peter 1:17-19).

Peter described the lives of people without Christ as "vain conversation." We, on the other hand, through our faith in Christ, have been redeemed from an aimless existence. Now we have a destiny calling and a calling destiny on our lives. Our redemption came at great cost. Silver and gold were not enough; they were of the earth and therefore corruptible. Nothing less than the "precious blood of Christ"—a treasure more priceless than any on earth—could pay our redemption price. As "the Lamb of God which taketh away the sin of the world" (John 1:29), Jesus Christ was the perfect sacrifice, "without blemish and without spot." (1 Pet. 1:19). His incorruptible blood alone possessed the power to redeem us.

Our salvation—our right standing with God—was bought with the precious blood of Christ. No greater ransom has ever been paid to buy someone's freedom. The Bible only calls a few things 'precious', and the blood of Jesus is one of them. His blood is precious, powerful, and awesome, and it has a voice that cries out on our behalf.

Even as the voice of Abel's blood cried out to God for justice, the voice of Jesus' blood cries out for us, saying, "Mercy, mercy, mercy." With that cry, the mercy and blessing of God fall on us, the blood of Jesus covers us, and the enemy cannot destroy us.

In Revelation 5:6, John describes a scene in heaven where he sees "a Lamb as it had been slain," yet is alive. This implies a freshly slain lamb, and therefore fresh blood. The blood of Jesus never dries up; it is always fresh. In the realm of the Spirit, His blood still speaks blessing today as it did 2,000 years ago. His blood continually speaks for us in the heavenlies. It cries out for our families, for our sons and daughters. It cries out for our nation. Jesus' blood cries out for all lost souls that they may come to know Him.

The blood that washed believers in the early church still washes us today. Two thousand years ago, Jesus took our sin, pain, and sickness with Him to the cross. His blood covered us so that we could live. Jesus Christ is our Passover Lamb.

A Battle of the Wills [2]

Passover, or *Pesach*, is the chief festival of the Jews, around which their entire system of faith and practice is built. Religious Jews date the national and spiritual birth of Israel to the time of the exodus, when Moses led the Israelites out of slavery in Egypt. Passover was the climax to a season of signs and wonders that God performed in Egypt to "persuade" Pharaoh to let his Hebrew slaves go. After the first Passover, the Egyptian ruler was so eager to get rid of the Israelites that he practically drove them from the land.

Here's how it happened. Moses went to Pharaoh and said, "The Lord says, 'Let My people go!' "

Pharaoh said, "No. Who is the Lord that I should let the Hebrews go? I won't do it."

---

2. Some information in this section regarding the plagues and Egyptian theology was taken from the following book: Robin Sampson, Robin and Linda Pierce, *A Family Guide to the Biblical Holidays*, (Heart of Wisdom Publishing, 2001), pp. 113-115.

God then sent on Egypt a series of 10 signs, each one more severe than the one before. This was His way of saying to the Egyptians, "Hello! I'm here. Don't mess with Me. You had better take Me seriously!"

Many Old Testament scholars agree that the 10 signs together attacked the entire religious and theological structure of Egyptian society. God's purpose here was not only to free His people from slavery, but to show the Egyptians that He was the one true God and mightier than all the so-called gods of Egypt. The 10 signs demonstrated clearly that God was the sovereign Lord of history, creation, and mankind. To the Egyptians, divine presence and the natural world were insepa-rably bound. Their religious beliefs were shaped by four fun-damental views.

First of all, Pharaoh himself was a god in the eyes of his people. Second, the Egyptians worshiped the Nile River. They depended on its annual flooding to irrigate their crops and ensure a good harvest. Third, the Egyptians held all animal life in great religious awe. To them, all animals symbolized the divine. Finally, they worshiped the sun. Chief among all the deities of Egypt was the sun god, Amun-Re.

Each of the 10 signs attacked one of these views to show that the God of Israel was sovereign. Pharaoh's defeat in his battle of the wills with the Lord struck a severe blow to the belief that he was a god. The first of the 10 signs—turning the waters of the Nile to blood—revealed that the river was *not* divine. God controlled the river and its waters. Even so, Pharaoh would not let the Israelites go.

The Egyptian religious awe for animals was stretched to the limit. In the second sign, God sent frogs—millions of them—to infest the land. They were everywhere! Frogs repre-sented the fertility god, Isis. The Egyptians could not walk or sit anywhere without crunching frogs. They would climb into bed and there they were: hundreds of hoppers all croaking "ribbit" in unison. They had frog legs, frog omelets, frog fritters, fried frogs—you name it—until frogs were coming out of their ears! Then, all of a sudden, the frogs died. The frogs that symbolized life to the Egyptians died by the millions. Heaps of dead frogs under the hot desert sun—whew! What a smell!

Did it work? No. Pharaoh still would not listen to God. So the Lord sent plagues of lice (representing Seth, the Egyptian god of the earth), and flies (symbolizing Baal-zebub, the "lord of the flies" and the god of Ekron). Try to imagine the maddening itch of lice everywhere on your body and in your clothes! Then, tiny stinging insects or biting flies that torment you wherever you go, getting into your ears, eyes, and mouth and under your clothes, swarming onto your food, settling into your water, and laying eggs everywhere!

Still Pharaoh would not budge. God then sent a disease that killed the Egyptians' cattle. The Egyptians believed that all animals were possessed by the spirits of the gods. The bull was especially sacred to them, and was linked to their god Apis. Only cattle belonging to the Egyptians were affected. The cattle of the Israelites remained healthy.

The next two plagues demonstrated God's sovereignty over nature. Boils broke out from head to foot on the Egyptians (but not the Hebrews). Body sores were considered a punishment for sin. Then, hail mixed with fire fell and killed both man and beast. Again, only the Egyptians were afflicted. The plagues of boils and hail were direct attacks on the sorcerers and shamans of Egypt who were believed to control physical healing, agriculture, and the weather.

By this time, everyone in Egypt except Pharaoh was ready to let the Israelites go. The Bible says that God hardened Pharaoh's heart. Despite everything that had happened, Pharaoh obstinately refused to give in.

Just when the Egyptians thought it couldn't get any worse, God sent millions upon millions of locusts to strip the land bare of any remaining plant life. With this sign, the Lord undeniably devastated the power of the Egyptian gods and shamans of agriculture.

Amun-Re, the sun god, did not escape either. In the ninth sign, God covered Egypt with a deep darkness for three days, proving that Amun-Re was no god at all.

The First Passover

Through all of this, Pharaoh stubbornly refused to release the Israelites. Several times he promised to do so, and then changed his mind after the latest plague went away. Finally, God sent the tenth and most severe sign of all—the death angel—to move through the land of Egypt, taking the life of every firstborn, whether of man or animal.

This plague struck the decisive blow against Egyptian religion. The Egyptians believed that each night the sun fought and defeated the snake, Apophis, who symbolized the darkness. In that way, day came anew after each night.[3] They also believed Pharaoh to be the incarnation of the sun. Three full days of darkness followed by death striking the firstborn at midnight proved Pharaoh's impotence as a deity and the fallacy of the entire system of Egyptian theology.

---

3.   Honeycutt, Roy L., *The Broadman Bible Commentary, Volume 1 (Revised)*, (Nashville: Broadman Press, 1973), p. 347.

To protect His chosen people from this final plague, God made provision for their deliverance:

Then Moses called for all the elders of Israel, and said unto them, Draw out and take you a lamb according to your families, and kill the passover lamb. And ye shall take a bunch of hyssop, and dip it in the blood that is in the basin, and strike the lintel and the two side posts with the blood that is in the basin; and none of you shall go out at the door of his house until the morning. For the LORD will pass through to smite the Egyptians; and when He seeth the blood upon the lintel, and on the two side posts, the LORD will pass over the door, and will not allow the destroyer to come in unto your houses to smite you. And ye shall observe this thing for an ordinance to thee and to thy sons forever (Exodus 12:21-24).

By spreading lamb's blood on the lintels and doorposts of their houses and then remaining inside throughout the night, the Israelites placed themselves "under the blood" and were protected from the angel of death. This Passover blood was a foreshadowing of the blood that Jesus, the Lamb of God, would pour out centuries later to cover the sins of men.

That same night, the Lord instituted a special meal of roasted lamb, bitter herbs, and unleavened bread that the Israelites were to eat while dressed and ready to go, because when their deliverance came it would come quickly. This Passover meal was observed annually as a celebration of their preservation as well as their liberation from slavery.

God's promise was open-ended. He did not flatly declare, "I am going to bless the Jews and curse the Egyptians." *Anyone* who obeyed the Lord's instructions and put blood on their lintels and doorposts would be delivered. The Egyptians themselves could have exercised faith in the Lord in this way and the death angel would have passed over them as well. Instead, they rejected the Word of the Lord, and the firstborn in every Egyptian household died.

On that first Passover night 3,500 years ago, lambs were slaughtered throughout Goshen, the region of Egypt where the Israelites lived. Using hyssop branches as brushes, they were dipped in blood and then the Jews stroked lamb's blood on the doorposts and lintels of their houses. Afterwards, they ate the special meal together quietly, dressed and waiting to depart the land after 400 years of slavery. As the Jews waited quietly inside their homes, safely "under the blood," the Lord went through the land looking for blood on the doorposts. On that historic night 3,500 years ago, every firstborn died in every house not covered by the blood. Wailing and mourning were heard throughout the land of Egypt.

Pharaoh quickly summoned Moses and told him to leave, along with all his people and their belongings. God gave His people favor in the eyes of the Egyptians, who showered them with precious items of gold and silver as they departed. That very night the wealth of the wealthiest nation in the civilized world was transferred and became the wealth of God's people. Moses led the children of Israel—probably 3 or 4 million of them—out of Egypt amid shouts of joy and celebration from those who were protected under the blood.

Thirty-five hundred years ago, lamb's blood brought protection, deliverance, and freedom to God's people. The first Passover looked ahead 1,500 years to the time when the blood of a better sacrifice—Jesus, the Lamb of God—would be spilled to take away the sins of the world. Because of the death of our Passover Lamb, we have salvation today. We have miracles, deliverance, and redemption; sanctification, celebration, and joy. Without that first Passover, there would be no Jewish nation and, therefore, no Jewish prophets, no Jewish Bible, and no Jewish Messiah. That means there would be no Jesus Christ of Nazareth, and without Christ there would be no salvation. Without Jesus, no one would come into right standing with God.

The Elements of Passover [4]

In the traditional Passover meal, or *Seder*, every food item has symbolic significance. *Charoset* is a mixture of chopped walnuts, wine, cinnamon, and apples. It represents the mortar the Hebrew slaves used between the bricks in building Egyptian cities, as well as the sweetness of a better life. *Karpas*, or fresh greens, usually parsley, represent new life for the Jewish people as well as the hyssop used to spread the lamb's blood on the doorposts. During the meal, the parsley is dipped in salt water, representing the salty tears of slavery.

The *Seder* meal also includes roasted eggs, which represent life and resurrection, and the shank bone of a lamb, symbolic of the sacrificial lamb offering. Bitter herbs, usually freshly-grated horseradish, reflect the bitter affliction of slavery. *Matzah*, or unleavened bread, symbolizes the haste with which the Israelites left Egypt, with no time to allow yeast to rise. Leaven is also a common biblical figure for sin. Unleavened bread, then, also represents the need to get rid of sin in one's life.

---

4. Some information in this section regarding the *Seder* meal was taken from Sampson, *A Family Guide to the Biblical Holidays*, pp. 124-126, 134.

During the course of the meal, each person drinks four cups of wine, representing freedom, deliverance, redemption, and release. These four cups are called, respectively, the cups of sanctification, judgment, redemption, and kingdom. A fifth cup of wine is poured and set at a special place at the table for the prophet Elijah, symbolizing that he would be welcome at the *Seder* table. Often, a child is given the privilege of opening the door so that Elijah can come in. Making a place for Elijah represents welcoming both the Messianic age and the anointing and power of the Holy Spirit into their lives.

According to tradition, the youngest child at the table asks four questions about why Passover night is different from all other nights. These questions form the framework for the *Seder* leader to share the Passover story:

1.   Why do we eat only unleavened bread on this night when all other nights we eat either leavened bread or matzah?

2.   Why do we eat only bitter herbs on this night when all other nights we eat all kinds of vegetables?

3.   Why do we dip our vegetables twice on this night when we do not dip our vegetables even once all other nights?

4.   Why do we eat our meal with all of us reclining on this night when on all other nights we eat our meals sitting or reclining?

One interesting feature of the *Seder* is a ceremony involving the *matzah* bread. The leader takes three pieces of *matzah*, two for blessing, and one to be broken, and places them inside a cloth container with three compartments called the *matzah tash*. The three pieces of *matzah* represent the unity of God in the Father, Son, and Holy Spirit. Taking the center piece of *matzah* (representing the Son), the leader holds it up for everyone to see, then breaks it in two. He places one half of the broken bread back into the *matzah tash* and wraps the other in a linen cloth. This linen-wrapped *matzah* is called the *Afikoman*. The leader then hides the *Afikoman*. This is a symbolic picture of Jesus, whose body was broken, wrapped in a cloth, and buried (hidden), to rise again three days later.

Every element of the *Seder* commemorates that first Passover night, when God delivered His people from slavery in Egypt. The Passover itself points to Jesus, the Passover Lamb, whose death delivered us from bondage to sin.

Jesus, Our Passover Lamb

We who know Christ as Savior and Lord can rejoice today because our Passover Lamb has come, and His blood has set us free. No longer are we slaves to sin; we can live lives of personal holiness in the power of the Holy Spirit. As Paul wrote to the church in Corinth:

> *Purge out therefore the old leaven, that you may be a new lump, as ye are unleavened. For even Christ our Passover is sacrificed for us: Therefore let us keep the feast, not with old leaven, neither with the leaven of malice and wickedness; but with the unleavened bread of sincerity and truth* (1 Corinthians 5:7-8).

In these verses, Paul uses the image of leaven, or yeast, as a symbol for sin and the old way of life before Christ. Now that "Christ our Passover" has been "sacrificed for us," we can "keep the feast...with the unleavened bread of sincerity and truth." This means that we can live the kind of life that pleases and honors the Lord. Sin no longer has the power to hold us back.

Sometimes we tend to take for granted what Jesus did for us when He went to the cross. On that fateful Friday, all the demons of hell attacked Jesus in an effort to destroy Him. From the Garden of Gethsemane, where He sweated drops of blood, Jesus was taken through a mock trial—a "kangaroo court"—where He was condemned falsely by the leaders of His own people. Turned over to the Roman authorities, He was condemned again and flogged to within an inch of His life. Following this, He was paraded in humiliation through the city of Jerusalem and out to "the place of the skull"—Calvary— where He was nailed to a rough wooden cross and suspended between two criminals. As the weight of the sin of the world bore down on Him, Jesus experienced total separation from His Father, and cried out, "My God, My God, why hast Thou forsaken Me?" (Matthew 27:46b).

During His earthly ministry, Jesus' favorite term to describe Himself was "the Son of man," which identified Him as a son of Adam, like all other human beings. Jesus, the Son of man, was also the Lamb of God who came to take all the sin and curses of the Adamic race upon Himself. Everything that was due us as sinners, Jesus took upon Himself as our Passover Lamb.

The prophet Isaiah spoke to this work of Christ on the cross centuries before it happened:

> *He is despised and rejected of men, a Man of sorrows and acquainted with grief: and we hid as it were our faces from Him; He was despised, and we esteemed Him not. Surely He hath borne our griefs, and carried our sorrows; yet we did esteem Him stricken, smitten of God, and afflicted. But He was wounded for our transgressions, He was bruised for*

our iniquities; the chastisement for our peace was upon Him, and by His stripes we are healed. All we like sheep have gone astray; we have turned every one to his own way; and the LORD hath laid on Him the iniquity of us all (Isaiah 53:3-6).

The day that we call "Good Friday" was a dark day for Jesus, but He knew that Sunday was coming. On Friday, Jesus took our sins upon Himself and died, but Sunday came, bringing resurrection and victory. Jesus bore our sicknesses and carried our pains so that we could be healed. He became total sin for us. This was according to the Father's will: "Yet it pleased the LORD to bruise Him; He hath put Him to grief: when Thou shalt make His soul an offering for sin, He shall see His seed, He shall prolong His days, and the pleasure of the LORD shall prosper in His hand" (Isaiah 53:10).

In the 3rd chapter of the Book of Galatians, Paul wrote:

Christ hath redeemed us from the curse of the law, being made a curse for us: for it is written, Cursed is every one that hangeth on a tree: That the blessing of Abraham might come on the Gentiles through Jesus Christ; that we might receive the promise of the Spirit through faith (Galatians 3:13-14).

Jesus became a curse for us so that we could be blessed. He was condemned so we could be redeemed. So He became a curse for you. *He died according to the law so that we could be made alive according to the Spirit.*

As with all lambs sacrificed on the altar, the Passover lamb had to be perfect, without spot, flaw, or blemish. Jesus, our Passover Lamb, was spotless, unblemished by sin. At 9:00 on the morning of the 14th day of the month of *Nisan*, the

Passover lamb was bound to the altar in the temple and put on public display. At the same time, our Passover Lamb was nailed to a cross and put on public display on Calvary.

At exactly 3:00 in the afternoon of that high holy day, the high priest ascended the altar and, to the sound of the shofar, cut the throat of the Passover lamb, declaring, "It is finished." At the same moment, on Calvary, our Passover Lamb cried from the cross, "It is finished!" and gave up His spirit. "It is finished" means, "It is paid in full." Our sin debt was paid in full with the blood of Jesus Christ, our Passover Lamb, who was sacrificed for us.

"This is What the Lord Did for Me"

One reason God instituted the Passover was to give His people a powerful and visible means of passing along the message of His power and faithfulness to succeeding generations. He states this explicitly in His instructions to Moses:

> *This day came ye out in the month Abib. And it shall be when the LORD shall bring thee into the land… that thou shalt keep this service in this month. Seven days thou shalt eat unleavened bread, and in the seventh day shall be a feast to the LORD. Unleavened bread shall be eaten seven days; and there shall no leavened bread be seen with thee, neither shall there be leaven seen with thee in all thy quarters. **And thou shalt show thy son in that day, saying, This is done because of that which the LORD did unto me when I came forth out of Egypt** (Exodus 13:4-8, emphasis added).*

I believe it is significant that God wanted His people to remember the Passover event and their liberation from Egyptian slavery in very personal and specific terms: "This is...that which the LORD did for *me*." It was important that they pass it on to their children so that each new generation would come to know the Lord for themselves.

The same is true for us today. As believers we each have a personal testimony to God's goodness and faithfulness, and to the power of the Passover Lamb to cleanse us from sin. God wants us to pass our testimony on to generation after generation so that the knowledge of Him becomes personal to each of our sons and our daughters so that they can take possession of the Passover Lamb for themselves.

Part of our calling as believers is to pass on a living testimony of what the Lord has done. Our children need to hear us say, "This is what the Lord did for me." Lost people need to hear us say it. When we give voice to our personal experience with the saving grace of God, we encourage others to believe that His grace is for them as well. The more we testify to the Lord's goodness to us, the more He will build up our testimony. He will continue to bless us, giving us even more to testify about. His hand will be over us in our lives, in our children's lives, in our homes, in our financial lives, in our business lives, and in our creative lives. In every aspect of life we will be able to say continually, "This is what the Lord has done and is doing in my life."

The Hebrew word for Passover, *Pesach*, means to pass over in the sense of protection. When we place our faith in Jesus, the Passover Lamb of God, we build a protection over ourselves, our families, and our households—a covering protection of blood. Blood is living tissue. Jesus Christ is the living Word of God. His blood has the power to cleanse sin and give us eternal life, but we must place ourselves under His blood. Before the living Word of God can make a difference in our lives, we must enter in and make Him our own. Another way to look at it is that we must humble ourselves, plunge into His blood, and allow Him to make us His own. When we do, all the blessings and promises that God made to His people become ours as well.

The Blessings of Passover

Our son Ben was miraculously healed of terminal kidney disease when he was only six months old. Even so, every year for the next several years he was attacked horribly. At around the same time every year a spirit of death attacked him physically, trying to kill him. When we finally realized what it was, we said, "You foul spirit of death, leave our home, and leave our son." Still, we had to battle it through.

One year Ben got so terribly sick with pneumonia that for days he could not keep anything in his stomach. We had already fought through the whole thing about his kidneys, and now it looked as though death was coming over him again. In my anguish I cried out, "God, what's the answer?"

The Lord directed me to Exodus 23:25: "And ye shall serve the LORD your God, and He shall bless thy bread, and thy water; and I will take sickness away from the midst of thee." I had never discovered this verse before. After I read it, I went over to Ben's bedside. The poor little guy couldn't even keep down bread or water. He was about four years old. I said, "Ben, say this with me: " 'Jesus is blessing my water and my bread and taking sickness away from my midst.' "

Ben said it with me, and together we entered into a season of claiming the Lord's promise. A few minutes later, God's healing power was ministered to him, and he was able to eat crackers and keep water down. He went on to a full and complete recovery. Ben's healing, like the Israelites' deliverance from Egypt, came through the power of the blood of Jesus and through His sacrifice as the Passover Lamb.

Once God freed the Israelites from Egyptian slavery, He led them into the wilderness and began to teach them how to be His people and to prepare them for entering the promised land. He also gave them a promise of the blessings that would be theirs if they obeyed and followed Him:

> *And it shall come to pass, if thou shalt hearken diligently unto the voice of the LORD thy God, to observe and to do all His commandments which I command thee this day, that the LORD thy God will set thee on high above all nations of the earth. And all these blessings shall come on thee, and overtake thee, if thou shalt hearken unto the voice of the LORD thy God: Blessed shalt thou be in the city, and blessed shalt thou be in the field. Blessed shalt be the fruit of thy body, and the fruit of thy ground, and fruit of thy cattle, the increase of thy kine, and the flocks of thy sheep. Blessed shall be thy basket and thy store. Blessed shalt thou be when thou comest in, and blessed shalt thou be when thou goest out. The LORD shall cause thine enemies that rise up against thee to be smitten before thy face: they shall come out against thee one way, and flee before thee seven ways. The LORD shall command the blessing upon thee in thy storehouses and in all that thou settest thine hand unto; and He shall bless thee in the land which the LORD thy God giveth thee. The LORD shall establish thee an holy people*

unto Himself as He hath sworn unto thee, if thou shalt keep the commandments of the LORD thy God, and walk in His ways. And all people of the earth shall see that thou art called by the name of the LORD; and they shall be afraid of thee (Deuteronomy 28:1-10).

The blood of the Passover Lamb makes all these blessings possible, but obedience to the Lord is the key to bringing them into our lives: "And all these blessings shall come upon you and overtake you *because you obey the voice of the Lord your God.*" When we obey God, He will bless us wherever we go, whether in the city or in the country.

Verse 4 says, "Blessed shall be the fruit of thy body." That refers to our children. The reference to the increase of produce, herds, cattle, and flocks, means that everything we lay our hands to financially or business-wise will prosper.

The blood of Jesus removes the curse. Everything becomes blessing for those who have been delivered by the blood and who walk in obedience. God told them, and tells us today, "Enter in." Because of the blood of Jesus we can enter in and receive the promise of the Holy Spirit.

As the children of Israel were delivered through the blood of the Passover lamb, their destiny was the promised land. They spent some time in the wilderness, but they were always headed for the land of promise. We, too, are destined for promise—we and our children—and that promise is the Holy Spirit. What does the Holy Spirit do? He brings us into the promises of God. Without the Holy Spirit, we cannot enter into the blessings of Abraham. The more we follow the Holy Spirit and listen to His voice, the more anointing and ability we will have to apprehend the blessings of God for ourselves, our children, our neighbors, our nation, and the whole world.

The message of Passover is not just for us. It has a global scope. Jesus is "the Lamb of God who takes away the sins of the world." He has redeemed us, and we are a blessed people. Those blessings are not for us alone, however. Our Lord has a heart for the nations. His desire is that we who are so blessed share those blessings with a cursed world so that all people who will can enter into the cleansing and delivering power of the blood of the Passover Lamb, Jesus Christ. Therein lies redemption for the world.

Chapter Three

REVELATION OF REDEMPTION

Although I grew up in southern Africa, I am of Indian ancestry. My family was Hindu, and we could trace our Hindu lineage by name back 800 years. As staunch Hindis, we believed in reincarnation and karma. We had no concept of being cleansed of our sins. Hinduism teaches that we each have to bear our karma—we have to carry the weight of our sin from one life into the next. The quality of our character in our current life will determine the nature of our next life when we are reincarnated.

For example, if you lived a bad or evil life as a human, you might come back as a dog. If you were a bad dog, you might return as a flea. It is a virtually endless (and hopeless) cycle of birth, death, and rebirth. The only glimmer of light in this system is the slight possibility that through a succession of lives filled with "good karma," a person can reach *nirvana*, an unconscious state where the soul is finally released from the seemingly endless cycle of rebirths.

For centuries, this deceptive belief system has trapped millions of people in spiritual darkness. Even today, Hinduism's confusing and clouded doctrines continue to clog the minds and blind the eyes of millions around the world. I know this is true, because I was once one of them. But if it were not for the grace of God, I would be one still.

Searching for Truth

I was born and raised in the Hindu faith, and as I grew older the weight of my sin—my karma—pressed down on me more and more. No matter how hard I tried, my life seemed empty, without purpose, and burdened with care. "Surely," I thought, "there is more to life than this. What am I missing?" Something in me hungered for revelation. I was looking for answers and could not seem to find them in the religion of my birth.

As a young man, I would walk four miles out of the way every day to visit the Hindu temple, where I would bow in worship before the idols. I asked the priests all kinds of questions, hoping to find answers for my longing, but I never did. My search led me through yoga and every branch of Hindu philosophy, but I did not find what I was looking for. My heart still hungered for the truth.

Everybody searches for truth. I have traveled all over the world and asked people in many nations the question, "How many of you want truth in your life?" Not once has anyone told me that they wanted a lie. People everywhere are hungry for truth. They are desperate to know that life means more than the meager emptiness of their current experience.

My search for truth was fruitless until one day, when I was about 16, a Southern Baptist missionary came to our door. She asked me for a drink of water, and when I returned with it, she gave me a New Testament. Immediately I began to read it. I had read many other books, including all kinds of "holy books" on Indian worship, but I had never read anything like this Bible. It was like nothing else I had ever encountered before. This book was alive! The words came to life on the page to me. It was the strangest thing, as though the author was looking over my shoulder as I read.

The more I read, the more the weight of my sin pressed down, and the more I struggled with what I read. Centuries of Hindu tradition had taught me that my sins could not be forgiven, but only worked out in the successive cycles of death and rebirth. As a Hindu, I was proud of that tradition. After all, my ancestors had died fighting for the Hindu faith.

In the pages of that New Testament, I encountered Jesus Christ, who was different from any other person I had ever seen or heard of before. In the Gospel of John, I read where Jesus said, "And ye shall know the truth, and the truth shall make you free" (John 8:32). That really caught my attention! Truth is what I was looking for! Jesus said that knowledge of the truth would bring freedom, but what was the truth?

I found out a few pages later. In the 14th chapter of John, Jesus stated it quite plainly: "I am the way, the truth, and the life: no man cometh unto the Father but by Me" (John 14:6). I stopped reading for a moment as the force of that statement hit home.

"Wow!" I thought. I had been looking for truth, and here was Jesus saying, "I am the truth." After years of searching everywhere else for the truth, I discovered that day that truth was a *Person* named Jesus Christ. Truth is not found in the dry philosophies of men. You can search for truth in Islam, Hinduism, Buddhism, Confucianism, Judaism, intellectualism, humanism, communism, socialism, capitalism, or any other kind of "-ism" or philosophy, but you will never find it. Truth is found only in the person of Jesus Christ.

Yet, there will always be people who, like Pontius Pilate, miss the truth when it is standing right in front of them. Jesus stood before Pilate, who looked directly at Him and asked, "What is truth?" (John 18:38); all the while, Truth was standing right in front of him. Truth is a person named Jesus Christ.

Receiving the Truth

As I read those words of Jesus, "I am the way, the truth, and the life," the Holy Spirit began working in my heart. The Spirit of wisdom and revelation came upon me and opened my eyes to understand that Jesus is the Truth. All of a sudden, all my traditions were dead. The traditions of men make the Word of God of no effect. Any tradition, religious or otherwise, that keeps us from experiencing and knowing the living Christ is a tradition that needs to be discarded.

I really struggled with this. On the one hand, I now knew that Jesus was the truth; He was the one I had been looking for. On the other hand, I knew that turning to Christ meant turning my back on my traditions. It meant turning my back on my family, my friends, my culture, and even my entire heritage. That was not easy. I remember crying one night and saying to the Lord, "God, it is so difficult. My brothers and sisters, my mother, my entire family, my friends; everyone will reject me if I do this!"

In the midst of my tears, in the intensity of this experience, I fell asleep. It must have been a kind of "waking sleep" because, as my head hit the table, I heard it hit and thought, "That's my head hitting the table." Suddenly, I found myself in a place I had never been before, where I heard the most wonderful music, its harmonies penetrating to the depths of my inner-most being. Every one of my senses—sight, smell, hearing, taste, and touch—were heightened and deeply engaged in everything around me. I was surrounded by perfection. Soon, I was led to a beautiful river, and I sensed in my spirit that it was the river of life.

As I sought to absorb everything that was happening, Jesus Christ walked in. Somehow, I knew it was Him without even being told. I was immediately struck by His eyes. Never before had I seen eyes so full of compassion. They looked as though He knew intimately every tear that had ever been shed—including mine. He put His hand on my shoulder and said, "My little brother." That's when I woke up.

My Bible was still open where I had been crying over it, but somehow it was now open to a different page. To this day I do not understand how it could have happened, but my Bible was now open to the 18th chapter of Luke, where the rich young ruler asks Jesus, "What shall I do to inherit eternal life?" (Luke 18:18) When Jesus tells him to sell his possessions, give the money to the poor, and follow Him, the man "was very sorrowful: for he was very rich" (Luke 18:23). This man walked away from Jesus because he thought the price for following Him was too high. I heard the Holy Spirit ask, "Are you going to be the same way?"

"No, Lord," I replied. At that moment I repented of my sins and received Jesus Christ as my Lord and my Savior. Immediately, all that weight of sin that I had been carrying went away, and I knew that I knew that I knew I was forgiven and had been born again.

One of our problems as Christians in America is that we have heard the phrase "born again" so often that we tend to take it for granted. In many ways we have forgotten what it really means to be born again. Our faith becomes tired and boring because we have lost sight of who we are. We need the impartation of God's revelation Spirit to remind us of who we are and what we have as born again believers: we are saved, God is our Father, heaven is our home, and Jesus is our elder brother—our Savior and Lord.

After I gave my life to Christ, I felt like Superman! I wanted to leap over tall buildings, stop trains, do *something*! My life changed completely, and I owe it all to the Lord. Without His wisdom and revelation that He imparted to me, I never would have understood the Scriptures, and I never would have come to know Christ.

Head-knowledge may make us smart, but it takes revelation to change our lives. I was destined to be a Hindu leader. Because I was a national debate champion and had written the best writings, I was being trained for leadership in the Hindu community. God intervened and changed my life forever. Through His Spirit of revelation, I came to know Jesus as my personal Savior. My sins were forgiven and my eternal destiny altered. I praise God every day for His mercy that gave me such life-changing revelation.

God's Progressive Self-Revelation

The God of the Bible is a self-revealing God. He chooses to make Himself known to us. Otherwise, we could never know Him. Our sinful nature blinds us to spiritual truth. Left to our own wisdom or discernment, God would remain unknown to us. If we have any hope of knowing God, it must come through His self-revelation.

Throughout the Bible we see the process of God progressively revealing Himself to people. Frequently, when a Bible character came to know God in a new way, he or she marked that occasion by assigning a new name to God—a name that reflects the new revelation.

For example, prior to the days of Moses, the Hebrews knew God generally as the "God of the Fathers." Within this broad classification, they referred to God by several different names, many in combination with the primitive Semitic name *El*, which is a generic term for God or deity.[5] One of these names is *El-Shaddai*, "God of the Mountains," or "Almighty God." According to Exodus 6:3, this is the name by which Abraham and the other patriarchs knew Him: "I appeared to Abraham, to Isaac, and to Jacob, as God Almighty (*El-Shaddai*), but by My name LORD (*Yahweh*) I was not known to them."

Yahweh is the personal or covenant name for God, the name He revealed to Moses at the burning bush.

Then Moses said to God, "Indeed, when I come to the children of Israel and say to them, 'The God of your fathers has sent me to you,' and they say to me, 'What is His name?' what shall I say to them?" And God said to Moses, "I AM WHO I AM." And He said, "Thus you shall say to the children of Israel, 'I AM has sent me to you.' " Moreover God said to Moses, "Thus you shall say to the children of Israel: 'The LORD [Yahweh] God of your fathers, the God of Abraham, the God of Isaac, and the God of Jacob, has sent me to you. This is My name forever, and

---

5.   Trent C. Butler, ed., *Holman Bible Dictionary*. (Nashville: Holman Bible Publishers, 1991), p. 1005.

this is My memorial to all generations' " (Exodus 3:13-15).

Through the years, the Jews gradually came to consider the name *Yahweh* too sacred to pronounce, so when they came to that name in Scripture, they substituted the word *Adonai* (LORD). Many English translations of the Bible continue that custom even today by rendering the Hebrew name *Yahweh* as "LORD" (in all caps, as in the above example).

To the patriarchs, God was known as *El-Shaddai* (Almighty God), or *El-Elyon* (Most High God), or *El-Roi* (God who sees me) or by other names. When God was ready to enter into covenant with His people, He revealed His personal covenant name, *Yahweh.*

Apparently, this was true even with Abraham, who lived centuries before Moses. Abraham knew God as *El-Shaddai,* but one day on Mount Moriah he came to know God in a new way. In a test of Abraham's faith, God had commanded him to offer his son Isaac as a burnt offering. Abraham obeyed. Just as he was ready to bring down the knife to slay his son, who was bound and lying on the altar, God stopped him and provided a substitute:

> *And He said, "Do not lay your hand on the lad, or do anything to him; for now I know that you fear God, since you have not withheld your son, your only son, from Me." Then Abraham lifted his eyes and looked, and there behind him was a ram caught in a thicket by its horns. So Abraham went and took the ram, and offered it up for a burnt offering instead of his son. And Abraham called the name of the place, The LORD Will Provide [Yahweh-Jireh]*

as it is said to this day, "In the Mount of the LORD [Yahweh] it shall be provided" (Genesis 22:12-14).

Before this event, Abraham knew God as *El-Shaddai* (Almighty God); afterward he also knew God as *Yahweh-Jireh* (God Who Provides).

In this way we can see a little of how God reveals Himself to us. The important thing to note here is that the *only* way we can come to know God is through His *self-revelation*. In the New Testament, God revealed Himself most fully in the person of His Son, Jesus Christ. When Philip said to Jesus, "Lord, show us the Father," Jesus replied, "He who has seen Me has seen the Father" (John 14:8-9).

The Spirit of Wisdom and Revelation

God wants to give all of us the spirit of wisdom and revelation so that the eyes of our hearts may be enlightened. He is not interested in our simply adding some new notes to the margins of our Bibles: "This is what the Lord showed me today." Whenever God reveals Himself to us, it is because He wants us to enter into a new experience with Him that will take us to a new level of understanding and spiritual maturity. God never gives revelation purely for its own sake. Revelation is always for the purpose of growth and the advancement of the purposes of God.

We receive revelation in many different ways. Often, it comes in answer to prayer. Another source of revelation is the Word of God. As we read and study the Bible, the Holy Spirit opens our minds and reveals the meaning of the Scriptures to us, and we come to know God and His ways at a deeper level. Sometimes revelation comes through a prophetic word. However revelation comes to us, we need to move into the energy or force of that revelation. When God imparts revelation, He wants us to enter into it, enjoy it, believe it, and experience it. With revelation comes experience.

God opens the doors of revelation for us, but the choice is ours whether or not we go in and experience it. There are always some who choose to stand outside rather than step through the door. Fear or unbelief or apathy keep them from entering. Every time we fail to act on revelation, we rob ourselves of an opportunity to know the Lord better and to be involved in His purpose. God is not interested in our standing around outside and observing. He wants us to participate with Him in His Kingdom work. God is always working. Whenever He reveals Himself, whenever He shows us where He is working, that is His invitation for us to join Him in what He is doing.

Jesus called and trained disciples for that very purpose. He revealed to them who He was, why He had come, and the nature of His work. Then He gave them His authority and commissioned them to do the same work He was doing. Here are just a few examples:

> *And when He had called His twelve disciples to Him, He gave them power over unclean spirits, to cast them out, and to heal all kinds of sickness and all kinds of disease....These twelve Jesus sent out and commanded them, saying: "Do not go into the way of the Gentiles, and do not enter a city of the Samaritans. But go rather to the lost sheep of the house of Israel. And as you go, preach, saying, 'The kingdom of heaven is at hand.' Heal the sick, cleanse the lepers, raise the dead, cast out demons. Freely you have received, freely give"* (Matthew 10:1, 5-8).

After these things the Lord appointed seventy others also, and sent them two by two before His face into every city and place where He Himself was about to go... "Whatever city you enter, and they receive you, eat such things as are set before you. And heal the sick there, and say to them, 'The kingdom of God has come near to you' "...Then the seventy returned with joy, saying, "Lord, even the demons are subject to us in Your name." And He said to them, "I saw satan fall like lightning from heaven. Behold, I give you the authority to trample on serpents and scorpions, and over all the power of the enemy, and nothing shall by any means hurt you" (Luke 10:1, 8-9, 17-19).

And He said to them, "Go into all the world and preach the gospel to every creature. He who believes and is baptized will be saved; but he who does not believe will be condemned. And these signs will follow those who believe: In My name they will cast out demons; they will speak with new tongues; they will take up serpents; and if they drink anything deadly, it will by no means hurt them; they will lay hands on the sick, and they will recover" (Mark 16:15-18).

And Jesus came and spoke to them, saying, "All authority has been given to Me in heaven and on earth. Go therefore and make disciples of all the nations, baptizing them in the name of the Father and of the Son and of the Holy Spirit, teaching them to observe all things that I have commanded you;

and lo, I am with you always, even to the end of the age" (Matthew 28:18-20).

Most assuredly, I say to you, he who believes in Me, the works that I do he will do also; and greater works than these he will do, because I go to My Father (John 14:12).

Do you see the progression? Jesus had authority from His Father. He gave that authority first to the 12 apostles, then to the 72 disciples. Finally, He imparted His authority to all believers—to everyone who bears His name. We have the same authority Jesus had, and that authority enables us in the power of the Holy Spirit to do "greater works" than Jesus did, because He went back to the Father.

The Book of Acts gives clear evidence that after Jesus ascended, His followers did indeed act with His authority and power. Peter healed a lame man (see Acts 3:1-9). Philip preached with power in Samaria and performed miraculous signs, including the casting out of unclean spirits and the healing of paralyzed and lame people (see Acts 8:5-8). Peter raised to life a woman named Dorcas who had died (see Acts 9:36-42). Paul cast a spirit of divination out of a slave girl (see Acts 16:16-18). Later, Paul brought back to life a young man named Eutychus, who had fallen to his death from a second-story window (see Acts 20:7-12).

The same authority that empowered these early disciples has been given to us—the spirit of wisdom and revelation.

Report What You See and Hear

Judging from the Book of Acts, everywhere the disciples of Christ went proclaiming the gospel, signs and wonders accompanied them to attest to the truth of their message. As a result, lost people by the thousands were redeemed from satan's kingdom of darkness and released into the freedom and light of the kingdom of God. To redeem means "to buy back at a price." The redemption price to set us free was the blood of Jesus, the Lamb of God.

As in those days, Jesus wants us to be a people who will do as He told the disciples of John the Baptist: "Go and tell...the things which you hear and see: the blind see and the lame walk; the lepers are cleansed and the deaf hear; the dead are raised up and the poor have the gospel preached to them" (Matthew 11:4-5).

Throughout my ministry I have been in countless miracle services. God has blessed me with the privilege of witnessing every healing miracle mentioned in the Bible. I have seen lepers cleansed; I have seen crippled people walk again; I have seen people born blind receive their sight.

Once I had the opportunity to present the gospel in Pakistan, and I remember seeing a woman who had been blind from birth. She was sitting all alone, one of the poorest of the poor in one of the poorest nations on earth. Her hands were clasped before her and her whole demeanor suggested the question, "Is there any hope for me?" I took a picture of her, because she represented to me all the millions of people in the world who sit in darkness, literally or spiritually, waiting for the light.

A little later, as I was declaring the gospel of the Lord Jesus Christ and the power of the Lamb of God, this same woman walked up. I looked at her face and said, "I see it, but I don't know whether I can believe it." Her eyes were whole and complete! She testified, "I was born blind, but now I can see. Jesus Christ has done this for me!"

When the Spirit and the Word combine together—when the power of God's Word combines with the presence of the Holy Spirit—I always urge people, "If you need a miracle, don't sit back. Get into the flow of God. Be humble enough to say, 'I need You, Lord.'"

Another time, when I was in Jamaica, the Lord gave me a special word about a lady in the audience. "There is a lady here," I said, "who is dying of cancer. Your doctors have given you only a couple more weeks to live. Stand up, because the Lord is going to heal you."

Indeed, a lady named Rosie stood up, stepped from her place, and started running to the front. When she came within about five feet, she suddenly fell down, and the anointing of God came and touched her. Her doctors in Kingston had all kinds of X-rays to prove that she was dying from lymphoma. Many of her bones had deteriorated. She was in severe pain and close to death. The power of God came upon her at that meeting and recreated her diseased bones overnight. When the doctors took some more X-rays, they were very puzzled.

"You are not the same woman," they told her. "Your bones have been completely restored. There is no sign of cancer anywhere."

Some time later I held a tent crusade in Jamaica, and there was Rosie on a chair in the front row, dancing before the Lord and saying, "Thank You, Jesus!"

One evening during those phenomenal meetings in Zaire, that I mentioned in Chapter One, people were lined up giving testimonies to their healings or other miracles. By that time I was so overwhelmed by what the Lord was doing, that I felt I couldn't listen anymore; it was just too much. I was sitting there writing and working on my notes in preparation for preaching the Word in a few moments, when I heard a commotion in the crowd. I looked up to see a man dressed in white, holding up his little boy. The crowd was going wild, so I turned to my interpreter and asked, "What was that?"

He replied, "That was a resurrection."

"What?" I asked, completely astounded.

"That was a resurrection," he repeated. He then interpreted the man's story for me.

"My son died this morning of cerebral malaria," the man said. "I took him to the clinic where he was declared dead several hours later. Then I remembered that someone had told me that the man of God was preaching here tonight."

He had walked 10 miles to the meeting, where he wrote out his prayer request and put it with the thousands of others there on the stage. I had laid hands on the pile of requests and prayed for them. During that time I had suddenly received a very specific and especially strong word from the Lord. I stopped in the middle of things and said, "The Lord has shown me that there is a man here whose son died this morning. The Lord wants me to tell you that this day He is going to do a great thing for you and for your son." As I felt the prompting of the Spirit, I prayed for the release of resurrection power. I had no idea what was going to happen or how, but God put the breath of life back into that little boy's body 10 miles away, and he was restored to life.

Jesus Christ is the same yesterday, today, and forever. In that one week alone, 118,000 people were born again out of a cumulative total of one and a half million who attended.

Truly, the redemption of the Lord Jesus was revealed and seen in that place.

Take It to the Nations

Lots of Christians today speculate about the return of Christ. When will He come back? How will He come back? Will it be soon? Jesus Himself gave us one clear clue to the general timing of His return: "And this gospel of the kingdom will be preached in all the world as a witness to all the nations, and then the end will come" (Matthew 24:14).

Although the specific timing of Christ's return is in the Father's hands, establishing the general atmosphere on earth for it is in ours. It has nothing to do with the devil or with the anti-christ. We will prepare the way for the return of Jesus as we are faithful in taking the gospel of the Kingdom to the nations. God wants to bring redemption to the people of the world, and He has called us to join Him in the task.

It is time for us as believers to rise up in faith and act on the revelation God has given us. Too often we let the devil or other people limit us or define who we are going to be, where we are going to go, and what we are going to do. Many times we listen to "religious" teaching rather than the instruction of the Holy Spirit. God is telling us, "Don't let the wisdom of man define what you do; let the Holy Spirit define what you do."

How does the Holy Spirit define our work? Listen again to the words of Jesus: "He who believes in Me, the works that I do he will do also; and greater works than these he will do, because I go to My Father" (John 14:12). Jesus made this statement in the context of promising His disciples to send the Holy Spirit. It is only in the presence and power of the Holy Spirit that we can fulfill the "Great Commission" of Matthew

28:18-20 to "make disciples of all the nations," and of Mark 16:15-18 to "go into all the world and preach the gospel to every creature" with signs and wonders following.

God wants us to have a vision, a revelation of the power of redemption through the Lord Jesus Christ. It is really a very simple message. We live in an age in which we are taught to believe that because the questions and challenges of life are confusing and complicated, the answers must be complicated as well. The more complicated something sounds, the more correct it must be. That's the way we think.

It is different with God. He doesn't think the way we do. " 'For My thoughts are not your thoughts, nor are your ways My ways,' " says the Lord. " 'For as the heavens are higher than the earth, so are My ways higher than your ways, and My thoughts than your thoughts' " (Isaiah 55:8-9). There is no way we could ever begin to comprehend all there is to God. Nevertheless, He has a way of presenting truth to us in very simple terms—the only way we can understand it.

Some folks are always trying to complicate the gospel of Christ by attaching all sorts of man-made restrictions or adding a lot of weird doctrines or couching it in language so complex and technical that even a person with a Ph. D. in English would scratch his head. God, on the other hand, has made the gospel so simple that even a child can understand it. Even very young children can comprehend sin and the fact that Jesus loves them, and say, "Jesus, I'm sorry for my sins; please come into my heart."

I've seen hundreds of children say something as simple and then be slain in the Spirit and start speaking in tongues. This may offend a lot of the theologians and religious scholars, but Jesus never said to a child, "You need to wait until you have a chance to go to Bible college or seminary and get a theology degree before I can do anything for you or you do anything for Me." The Lord can use anybody of any age who is willing to humble himself or herself and follow Him. The gospel of Christ is simple, but at the same time mighty, glorious, and deep. The simple things of God are profound.

What could be simpler than, "Christ, our Passover, was sacrificed for us" (1 Corinthians 5:7)? He is the Lamb of God, and His blood avails for us. The blood of Jesus is sufficient for us, our children, our churches, our neighborhoods, our cities, and all the nations of the world. Remember that all it takes is one drop of the precious blood of Jesus to destroy the kingdom of satan. God has revealed redemption to the world, and it is found in the bleeding form of the Son of God hanging on a cross.

Let us not be ashamed of who we are or of the message we bear. God is saying to us, "Do not be afraid. Rise up in faith right now and take My revelation of redemption to the world." God wants to pour forth His power and His anointing to redeem families, cities, states, and nations. As Paul says, "[God] desires all men to be saved and to come to the knowledge of the truth" (1 Timothy 2:4). Every soul is precious in His sight.

Chapter Four

THE PEARL OF GOD

What's the value of a new BMW? Not long ago, the German automaker introduced a new model in its line of fine luxury cars. The general list price for the new car was around $84,000. Is that a good price? Is the vehicle worth it? How can you tell?

Suppose your local BMW dealer has just received the first vehicle of this new model in his showroom. It is the only one on his lot. Now suppose that you want to buy it but feel you shouldn't have to pay more than $65,000. What do you do? You might try going to the dealership and negotiating for that price. Depending on your skills as a negotiator and the circumstances of the dealer, you might even get it.

On the other hand, suppose it is a very popular model, and people are standing in line for it. Suppose further that a local millionaire businessman comes in and, without breaking a sweat, offers $250,000 cash for the car. Between you with your $65,000 and the businessman with his quarter of a million, who do you think the salesman will go with?

That question is a no-brainer! So then, what is the *real* value of that BMW? Is it the $65,000 you are willing to pay, the $84,000 the dealer is asking, or the $250,000 the businessman has offered?

What is the value of human life? An abortion-rights advocate would give you one answer while a pro-life activist would give you another. People who see the divine image in humanity would answer the question very differently from those who view mankind as merely the end product of a long and random evolutionary process.

To find the truth, we need to look to God. As Creator, He knows more about us than we know about ourselves. What value does God place on our lives? The answer to that question should be of supreme interest to us. Simon Peter states it pretty clearly:

> *You must know [recognize] that you are redeemed [ransomed] from the useless [fruitless] way of living inherited by tradition from [your] forefathers, not with corruptible things [such as] silver and gold, but [you were purchased] with the precious blood of Christ, the Messiah, like that of a [sacrificial] lamb without blemish or spot* (1 Peter 1:18-19, AMP).

Paul told the Corinthians, "You have been redeemed, at tremendous cost" (1 Corinthians 7:23, Phillips).

In one sense, the value of a thing is determined by how much the highest bidder is willing to pay. The millionaire was willing to pay a quarter of a million dollars for the prestige of having the first of the new BMW model in town so he could drive around and show it off to his friends and neighbors. To him, it is worth every penny he paid.

What is our value to God? How much was He willing to pay? God purchased us at a cost greater than we can truly comprehend: the lifeblood of His Son. All of the world's known reserves of gold, silver, diamonds, emeralds, and other precious metals and gems put together cannot compare to the value God places on *one* human soul.

How much are you worth to God? The devil will try to convince you that you are nothing but a failure who has fallen too far and sinned too much for God to care about anymore. Don't believe satan's lies. Jesus purchased you with His precious blood, more precious than anything on earth. He paid the highest possible price for you, and for all of us. Corporately, as believers, we are the ~~Bride~~ BODY of Christ. Jesus paid the ~~bride~~ price for us, and that price was His own blood.

The Richest People in the World

According to *Forbes* magazine's annual "Forbes 400" listing, Bill Gates of Microsoft® Corporation is the richest person in America and has been for the last decade or so. He and a handful of others, such as investor Warren Buffett and the heirs to the fortune of Sam Walton of Wal-Mart® Corporation, possess material wealth that staggers the imagination of most of us. Nevertheless, in spite of their financial prosperity, they are not truly the richest people in the land. Material wealth *alone* does not make *anyone* truly rich.

The richest people in America, and indeed, the world, are those who know Jesus, those who have seen the kingdom of God and have come to understand the true value of their souls. Once you know what your soul is worth, once you know how much God really thinks of you, you will know that you could pile all the wealth of the earth on one side of God's balance scale and stand by yourself on the other side, and the balance would tip in your favor. You, I, and every one of us individually are more valuable to God than all the wealth and treasures of the world put together.

Jesus said, "For what will it profit a man if he gains the whole world, and loses his own soul? Or what will a man give in exchange for his soul?" (Mark 8:36-37). Our soul is more important than anything the world has to offer. Nothing on this earth is worth trading our soul for.

We need revelation to understand this. That is why so many people in the world spend so much time pursuing earthly things and so little time tending to matters of the spirit. They have no revelation. Revelation is different from head-knowledge. Head-knowledge will make you smart, but it won't affect your heart. When God gives you revelation of His Word, it is a living truth that penetrates to the innermost core of your being and changes you from the inside out. Nothing and no one, whether hell or death, satan or demons, can take that revelation away.

God loved us enough to send His only begotten Son—His unique Son—to die in our place as payment for our sin. Jesus loved us enough to give His life willingly on the cross so that we might be forgiven and receive eternal life. Such love is truly incomprehensible. Although we cannot fully understand it, we can take it on faith and simply believe that it is true. God wants us to know that He loves us and to rest secure in that knowledge.

Paul's letter to the Ephesians could be called a "love letter" to the church. Part of the apostle's theme is the love of Christ for His church. In the 3rd chapter, Paul lifts up a prayer for his readers (including us):

For this reason I bow my knees to the Father of our Lord Jesus Christ, from whom the whole family in heaven and earth is named, that He would grant you, according to the riches of His glory, to be strengthened with might through His Spirit in the inner man, that Christ may dwell in your hearts through faith; that you, being rooted and grounded in love, may be able to comprehend with all the saints what is the width and length and depth and height; to know the love of Christ which passes knowledge; that you may be filled with all the fullness of God (Ephesians 3:14-19).

As followers of the Lord Jesus Christ, we are members of the "family"—God's family. Because we are God's children, we have access by right to the "riches of His glory." One of these riches is the presence of the Holy Spirit dwelling in our hearts. Notice that we cannot make room for "Christ to dwell in [our] hearts through faith" until we are "strengthened with might through His Spirit in the inner man." It is only by the Spirit's power that we are able to exercise the faith through which Christ comes to dwell in our hearts.

Why did the Father give us the Spirit to strengthen us in our inner man and Christ to dwell in our hearts through faith? He did it so that we would be "rooted and grounded in *love*" and "able to comprehend...the width and length and depth and height" of "the love of Christ." In other words, God gave us His Spirit and sent His Son to redeem us so that we might know His love. The love of Christ "passes knowledge," which means that it is impossible to understand by natural human reason. God's love must be spiritually discerned, and it is the Holy Spirit who gives us that discernment.

Another word for discernment that comes from the Spirit of God is *revelation*. It is by revelation alone that we know of God's love for us. People outside the Judeo-Christian tradition have no conception of a God who loves them personally. The idea is completely foreign to them. Without revelation, they will never know the God of love. All of us who know Christ used to be the same way. The Lord revealed Himself to us and brought us to faith. Now He wants to use us to reveal Himself to others so that they too can know His love as we do.

Field of Dreams

During His earthly ministry, Jesus taught by using parables. A parable is a simple story that uses familiar objects and language to teach profound truth. Someone once defined a parable as "an earthly story with a heavenly meaning." In the 13th chapter of his gospel, Matthew records two parables of Jesus that teach the magnitude and depth of God's love for us.

The first parable involves a treasure hidden in a field.

Again, the kingdom of heaven is like treasure hidden in a field, which a man found and hid; and for joy over it he goes and sells all that he has and buys that field (Matthew 13:44).

Try to imagine the scene: a man is walking in a field, an ordinary field with nothing to distinguish it from any other. Somehow, he accidentally discovers a great treasure in the field. Perhaps he had come across an old map that told him that treasure was buried here. Whatever the means, this man locates the treasure. Suddenly, an otherwise ordinary field has become priceless in his eyes. Hurriedly, he re-hides the treasure and

rushes off to purchase the field, even selling all his possessions in order to raise the money.

There is perhaps more than one way to understand this
parable. Many believers interpret the hidden treasure as the
kingdom of God, and the field as the world. When a man discovers the kingdom of God, he is willing to give up all he has
in order to possess it.

Although that is certainly a valid interpretation, I would
like to approach the story from a slightly different angle. The
field represents the world, and the man walking in the field is
Jesus Himself. From this perspective, the treasure represents
the people of God *in* the world. Jesus came in to the world
looking for people to redeem out of the world into His Father's
Kingdom. Those people are the treasure hidden in the field.
Finding them, and understanding their priceless value, Jesus
willingly gives up everything—including His very life—in
order to gain possession of the treasure.

Consider the details. When the man in the parable discovers the treasure, what does he do? He wisely keeps it hidden until he has a chance to buy the field. Otherwise, word of
the treasure might get out and suddenly there would be a lot of
competition for that otherwise worthless field. The man sells
everything he has and buys the field. Does he really want the
field? Probably not; he wants the *treasure* that is hidden there.
To get the treasure, he has to buy the field. Does he begrudge
the price he has to pay? No, because he knows the worth of the
treasure.

One of my favorite stories in high school was *The Count
of Monte Cristo*, which is about a young man imprisoned for
many years for political reasons. While in prison, he meets a
monk who confides in him the secret of a great treasure hidden

on a particular island. Released from prison as a middle-aged man, he goes in search of the treasure, finds it, and returns home richer than his wildest dreams. It's a tremendous story. There is joy and danger when you find treasure because there is so much you can do with it, for good or evil.

Appearances can be deceiving. We may have to penetrate beneath the surface to find the true value of something. People may have asked questions when the man in Jesus' parable sought to buy the field. "Why do you want *that* field? It's full of thorns. The soil is so bad that nothing useful can grow there. It's worthless." The man persists, however, because he knows the true worth that lies below the surface.

Jesus knows our true worth as well. He looks beyond the surface of our sin and failure and rebellion against God and sees precious treasure: lives ripe to be redeemed and bought back for the kingdom of God. "For God so loved the world that He gave His only begotten Son, that whoever believes in Him should not perish but have everlasting life" (John 3:16). God loved the world (the *people* of the world) so much that He gave the life of His Son. What does God get in return? He gets all the "whoevers"—all who will believe and trust Christ as Lord and Savior—to be in intimate relationship and fellowship with Him forever. The treasure in the field represents the total company of believers—all the "whoevers"—of every generation of man.

Jesus gave His life to purchase for Himself a people of His very own. Paul makes reference to "our great God and Savior Jesus Christ, who gave Himself for us, that He might redeem us from every lawless deed and purify for Himself His own special people, zealous for good works" (Titus 2:13b-14).

We are the treasure of Christ, the people who are His very own. He redeemed us from the world and from wickedness, purifying us with His blood, which was the price of our redemption. He cleaned us up and set us forth to shine with the glory of our Father. Now He wants us to work with Him in finding and digging up (liberating) more of His precious treasure buried in the field (the world), and helping to clean them up so they, too, can shine with the light of God.

The Most Precious Pearl

Jesus' second parable on God's love in the 13th chapter of Matthew immediately follows the first one and is closely related to it:

> *Again, the kingdom of heaven is like a merchant seeking beautiful pearls, who, when he had found one pearl of great price, went and sold all that he had and bought it* (Matthew 13:45-46).

This time, instead of a man in a field, there is a merchant searching the jewelry market. Instead of a great treasure, there is one exquisite pearl of great price. This merchant is not just a "window shopper," but an expert in precious jewels. He knows the worth of gems and knows exactly what he is looking for. One day he comes across a pearl unlike any other he has ever seen. Knowing the priceless value of his find, he quickly sells everything he has and buys that one pearl.

Again, let's consider the merchant to represent Jesus, the marketplace (implied in the parable) is the world, and the pearl of great price, the people of God. To make it even more personal, think of the one pearl as representing each individual person. Each one of us is so personally valuable to the Lord, that He would willingly give everything He had to redeem each of us alone. In other words, if you were the only person on earth who needed to be redeemed, Jesus would still have come to earth to die for your sins. The same is true for me or for anyone else.

I heard a true story some years ago about a man browsing in a flea market in Arizona. On one table he saw several piles of semi-precious stones, each pile priced at rock-bottom prices such as $3.00 or $5.00. Examining the stones, he finally selected one pile and bought it for about $3.50. His selection was not random. He had seen one particular stone in the pile that caught his interest.

After he got home, he examined the stone more closely and found that it was as he had suspected: one of the most perfect emeralds he had ever seen, worth several million dollars. This man was an expert jeweler, who knew what he was looking at. What others passed off as junk, he recognized as a treasure of great worth.

That's the way Jesus is. He knows the value that lies below the surface. The treasure in the first parable is *all* of God's redeemed people everywhere, the company of "whoevers" who have said "Jesus, I love You, and receive You as my Savior." Jesus wanted to give an even more specific picture, so He told of the merchant and his one pearl of great price that he gave everything for. *You* are that pearl. *I* am that pearl. Every individual who believes in Jesus is that pearl. With this story, Jesus is saying to us, "I gave everything I had for you. Now you are Mine, and no one can take you away from Me."

That's how Jesus looks at each of us. We are precious to Him, like the most precious pearl in the world, only more so. If you were the only person in the world who needed to be redeemed, Jesus would still say, "It was worth it to Me to give up all the riches of heaven, just so I could have you." How could there be any greater love than that?

No matter who you are or where you are from, no matter what your background, your past, or what other people may think of you, when Jesus looks at you, He sees a pearl. Your past is not what matters. Jesus is not so much concerned with where you have been as with where you are going. What matters is who you are now because of the blood of Christ, and who you are becoming in the power of the Holy Spirit.

Wherever I have traveled around the world, one of the common elements I have found is that people everywhere feel worthless. Life seems so harsh and unfair, and they wonder if they really matter. Many live under repressive regimes or unresponsive or incompetent governments and endure hunger, sickness, and poverty as regular facts of life. In many third-world countries, particularly in Africa, sorcery, demon possession, and occultic practices of all kinds are very prevalent and hold many of the people in the bonds of fear, ignorance, and spiritual darkness.

All of these people are precious pearls in Jesus' eyes, and He paid the price for their redemption 2,000 years ago when He gave His life on the cross. Their ransom has been paid, but many of them do not know it because no one has ever told them. That is where we come in. Now that Jesus has redeemed us, He wants us to take the good news of His redemption to those who do not know, so that they too can find freedom in Christ. Paul wrote:

> *How then shall they call on Him in whom they have not believed? And how shall they believe in Him of whom they have not heard? And how shall they hear without a preacher? And how shall they preach*

unless they are sent? As it is written: "How beauti-
ful are the feet of those who preach the gospel of
peace, who bring glad tidings of good things!"
(Romans 10:14-15).

We are pearls of great price in Jesus' eyes, and He paid
full price for us: His own lifeblood as the Lamb of God who
takes away the sin of the world. He will not be satisfied until
every pearl, every piece of His hidden treasure, has been
found, brought home, and cleaned up.

Paid in Full

In the 5th chapter of Revelation, John sees a vision of heav-
en where four "living creatures" and 24 "elders" are worshiping "a Lamb as though it had been slain" (Revelation.
5:6,8).

And they sang a new song, saying: "You are worthy
to take the scroll, and to open its seals; for You were
slain, and have redeemed us to God by Your blood
out of every tribe and tongue and people and
nation, and have made us kings and priests to our
God; and we shall reign on the earth" (Revelation
5:9-10).

For many people, the word "redemption" is nothing more
than a religious term with little practical meaning. In reality, it
is a very powerful word that originated in the ancient business
world. For example, it was used in the slave markets to refer
to the price paid either to purchase a person or to purchase that
person's release.

In New Testament days, when a bill was paid or a purchase completed, the bill of sale was stamped with the Greek
word τελέω (*teleo*), which means "paid in full." Even today,

when we pay off a debt we sometimes receive a receipt or promissory note with "Paid in Full" stamped on it. Jesus used a form of the word τελέω (*teleo*) in John 19:30 when He said from the cross, "It is finished," meaning that the sin debt of mankind had been paid in full by His death.

What does it mean for us that Jesus paid our sin debt in full? For one thing, it means that no one else can lay claim to us anymore. We belong to Jesus and are forever free from satan's grasp. The devil can harass us and tempt us, but he can never again take ownership of our soul. Jesus bought us with His blood and we are forever His.

It is like seeing a house with the real estate agent's sign in the front saying, "For Sale," and then driving by a couple of weeks later and seeing the word "Sold" attached to the sign. "Sold" means no one can make a bid on that house anymore. The papers of ownership have been signed and the buyer has paid the price. No one else can claim that house. It is τελέω (*teleo*), "paid in full."

Like a benevolent trader at a slave market, Jesus can buy our release from bondage because He has already paid the price. No one can contest His right of ownership. If anyone demands to see a bill of sale, all He has to do is show them the nail prints in His hands and feet or the spear thrust in His side. No one can lay a hand on us because our freedom has been paid in full on the authority of the blood of Jesus.

Sometimes we as believers live and act as if we do not realize that Jesus has paid our debt in full. We play around and get wishy-washy with our lifestyle, sometimes living for God, and sometimes living like the devil. Once we truly understand what "paid in full" means, we will no longer have any question about whom we serve! We belong to Christ and He has the right to our absolute allegiance and obedience. We owe Him every-thing, and nothing less than our all is worthy of Him.

The more we understand this revelation that we are pre-cious pearls of God bought and paid for in full by the blood of Jesus, the more powerful and effective that revelation will be in our lives. We will learn to walk more and more in the full authority that we have in Christ and will experience victory in daily living to an increasing and greater degree.

A Contract Written in Blood

Redemption is a mighty and awesome truth, the greatest news the world has ever heard. Even when as a human race we were "dead in trespasses and sins" (Ephesians 2:1), God loved us and sent His Son to redeem us—to purchase our freedom—with His own blood. Jesus brought us from death to life. This blessing is not for us alone, but for our children and succeeding generations. The blood that Jesus shed on the cross is sufficient to redeem every man and woman and boy and girl on the planet—past, present, and future.

Because Jesus has redeemed us, we no longer live for ourselves alone. Romans 14:8 says, "For if we live, we live to the Lord; and if we die, we die to the Lord. Therefore, whether we live or die, we are the Lord's." We have been bought with a price. Now we belong to Jesus, and we need to remember the seriousness and the magnitude of the price He paid. It wasn't like negotiating the price of a new BMW. When Jesus set out to redeem us, He paid the most awesome and costly price in history. Nothing in either the physical or spiritual realms is more valuable than the blood of Jesus.

The more we learn to honor the blood of Jesus and what He did for us, the more effective the power of His blood will become in our individual lives, our families, our churches, our nation, and our world.

In Jesus we are under a new covenant, a contract with God signed in the blood of Jesus and sealed in our hearts with His Spirit. The apostle Peter wrote that Jesus "Himself bore our sins in His own body on the tree, that we, having died to sins, might live for righteousness; by whose stripes you were healed. For you were like sheep going astray, but have now returned to the Shepherd and Overseer of your souls" (1 Peter 2:24-25). Jesus died for our sins that we might have new life, abundant and eternal. He became sin for us that we might become the righteousness of God in Him.

This new life is the supernatural life of God, the *zoe* life flowing in us. People without Christ have only the biological life and breath; the spiritual part of them is dead, because it comes alive only in Christ. Because of Christ, we who are believers are different from "regular" people. This is not a source of pride for us, but a demonstration of God's mercy toward us. He has given us *zoe* life, and what He has given us, He desires all people everywhere to receive. We who have received God's saving, redeeming mercy have the responsibility from Him to be merciful to others and to share with them the good news of His mercy and redeeming grace through the blood of Christ.

We are children of a new covenant signed in Jesus' blood. This is a very solemn and powerful covenant, the kind that the Bible calls a *blood covenant*, which we will learn more about in the next chapter.

Chapter Five

REVELATION OF THE BLOOD COVENANT

Today a great battle is underway for the soul of our nation. We are in danger of forgetting who we are as Americans and where we came from. In many parts of our country, basic civil and religious liberties are under attack in the name of political correctness, diversity, tolerance, and multiculturalism. The traditional concept of the family is maligned while sodomy is given constitutional protection.

A California court declares that the phrase "under God" in the Pledge of Allegiance is unconstitutional. In Alabama, a monument depicting the Ten Commandments is forcibly removed from the rotunda of the state capitol and hidden in a storeroom. Such a monument, said a U. S. Circuit Court, is an unconstitutional mixing of church and state. (It doesn't seem to matter that the Ten Commandments are the basic foundation for the entire system of law in the United States.) The chief justice of the Alabama Supreme Court, who sponsored the monument and adamantly defied the Circuit Court's ruling, is suspended because of his stance.

We in America are in danger of losing the meaning of certain things that traditionally have been dear and precious to our culture, our national identity, and our way of life. When I was in college, some of my friends joined the Marines and ended up in Vietnam. I was tempted to go with them, but I had made a commitment to school, and my pastor persuaded me that school was my top priority. So, while some of my buddies were fighting for their country in Southeast Asia, I finished college.

Some of my friends who went to Vietnam were wounded in action, and a few even died. Like so many other young men and women, they served their country faithfully, regardless of what their personal feelings may have been about that conflict. I remember how so many of our soldiers returned to the United States after their tour in Vietnam only to be greeted on their arrival by jeers and ridicule. They were spat upon, cursed, and called "baby killers" and worse by people who were adamantly, loudly, and sometimes violently opposed to the war.

Such a hostile reception did deep injury not only to those returning soldiers, but also to our national consciousness and identity as a people. By cheapening what these servicemen and servicewomen were willing to do for their country, we cheapened ourselves as a nation.

The 1970s was a low period for our national morale, but some things have begun to turn the corner in the years since. For example, soldiers who served in the Persian Gulf War in 1991 and the Iraq war in 2003 have returned home to receive a hero's welcome. I recently read a piece about the funeral of a young soldier from a small town in Texas who was killed in action in Iraq. The article, written by his aunt, described a service that fittingly honored a fallen hero, a service attended by over 1,000 people.

More amazing than the service itself was what happened on the way to the cemetery. Cars along the highway not only pulled to the side of the road, but the drivers and passengers got out and stood quietly as the processional went by. Some even waved small flags. Store owners and customers, construction workers, and others along the route stood silently in respect for the young man who had given his life for his country.

When the processional turned off the highway onto the street leading to the cemetery, it was greeted by lines of young boys on both sides of the street holding American flags with one hand, and their other hand on their hearts. Even elementary school children and their teachers turned out. At the cemetery, several high-ranking military officers, including two generals, as well as a color guard and representatives from every branch of the service were on hand to honor the fallen hero.

Perhaps we are starting to regain some of the sense of honor and dignity that the enemy tried to steal from our hearts as a nation. Perhaps we are beginning to rediscover the meaning of sacrifice. We face an ongoing battle to retain in our hearts the meaning of some of the basic foundational things that we believe in—principles that make us who we are, and that make us great, honorable, and special as a people, both individually and collectively.

A Better Covenant

One of the principles of life is that the things we cease to value we will eventually lose. Once we no longer understand why something is important, we no longer have a reason to hold onto it tightly. This is true not only for a nation, but for the people of God as well. There are some biblical concepts that many Christians today do not place much value on either because of ignorance or cultural distance. What I mean is that we either have not been taught the importance of these concepts, or we fail to appreciate their value because they arose in a culture foreign to our own. One of these important biblical concepts is the principle of the *blood covenant*.

As children of God, we are by nature a covenant people. A covenant is often compared to a contract, but biblical covenant goes much deeper. Generally, a contract is limited to the *legal* obligations between parties. Covenant touches moral and spiritual obligations.

The Bible tells how God has related to His people through two covenants: the old covenant (testament) with Abraham and his descendants, and the new covenant (testament) through Christ. Why were there two covenants? The new covenant in Christ fulfilled the old covenant and accomplished some things the old covenant could not do.

Speaking of Jesus, the writer of Hebrews said:

But now He has obtained a more excellent ministry, inasmuch as He is also Mediator of a better covenant, which was established on better promises. For if that first covenant had been faultless, then no place would have been sought for a second (Hebrews 8:6-7).

Jesus is the "Mediator of a better covenant." Why is it better? It is better because Jesus *makes* it better. The first covenant was merely type and shadow; the new covenant is the "real deal." The old covenant had no Jesus; in the new covenant, Jesus is the central character. The old covenant had only the blood of animal sacrifices, which could never take away sin; the new covenant has the precious, priceless blood of Jesus Christ, the Lamb of God, who takes away the sin of the world.

Covenant is very much an Eastern concept. The more we have Westernized it, the more we have lost its meaning. To understand covenant, we must look to its origins as an Eastern—and specifically Hebraic—concept as opposed to a Western theological idea or legal transaction.

The Hebrew word for covenant is *beriyth*, which comes from a very ancient root that means "to fetter." Words with a similar meaning include "confederacy," "compact" (as in: to make a compact with someone), and "league," (as in: being in league with someone). In its Hebrew form, *beriyth* also stems from a word meaning "to cut," from the practice of covenant parties passing between them cut pieces of meat in making the covenant. More precisely, *beriyth* means "to cut until bleeding occurs." The cut must be deep enough for blood to flow. Blood, then, is at the very heart of the meaning of covenant.

The Eastern mind regards blood quite differently than the Western mind. From the Hebraic perspective as revealed and established in the Bible, without blood, there is no covenant. When Eastern men, Hebrews or otherwise, drew up a contract, they would seal it by "cutting" a covenant. The covenant was a guarantee that neither party would back out of the agreement, and it was sealed in blood. "No blood, no covenant."

Four Ways of Sealing a Blood Covenant

Generally, there were four ways to enter into a blood covenant in the Eastern tradition. The first was to cut the palm of one hand of each party until blood began to flow into the palms, then the palms were brought together so the blood could mingle. That was "cutting a covenant," and the parties participating became blood brothers.

One of my favorite movies is *The Outlaw Josey Wales*, starring Clint Eastwood. At one part of the story, the character Josey Wales makes friends with an Indian chief named Lone Watie. To seal their friendship, they strike a blood covenant. Josey Wales takes out his knife and makes a cut on his palm. Lone Watie does the same. Then, they bring their hands together, mingling their blood, thus becoming blood brothers.

This act brought a bond deeper than simple friendship. Becoming blood brothers was like becoming part of the same family. At the very minimum, it meant that Josey Wales and Lone Watie and their people would never make war on each other. In addition it meant that each would come to the other's aid if needed. If Josey Wales was in trouble, Lone Watie would help him. If Lone Watie was in a tight spot, Josey Wales would come to his aid. Blood brotherhood was a lifelong relationship as strong as biological family ties and just as irreversible.

That is what blood covenant is all about: a lifelong commitment between people or parties for their mutual welfare that overrides all other considerations.

Today, the handshake is the visual lingering remnant of this form of sealing a blood covenant. My wife, Bonnie, grew up in New Mexico where her father served as a sheriff in the 1960s. He used to tell me about some of the traditions they grew up with. For example, in the West, ranchers would make an agreement such as, "You can use my water" or, "You can cut through my property," and then they would say, "Let's shake on it," and they would shake hands. That handshake was like a holy thing to them. They were entering into a covenant, and they took it very seriously. Character was critically important, and a man's word was his bond.

A second way of sealing a blood covenant, similar to the first, was for each person to make a cut on his own wrist and then to bring their wrists together with the other person's so their blood could mingle. Notice that both of these cases involve a mingling of the blood. By so doing, the parties cutting the covenant became "one blood."

Another Eastern tradition for sealing a blood covenant involved, again, cutting the hand or the wrist to let blood flow. Each person would then take several drops of his blood and put it in a cup filled with wine, and they would share the cup. In this way, each person indicated his willingness to enter into covenant with each of the others.

The final way to seal a blood covenant was to sacrifice an innocent animal and let its blood substitute for the blood of those who were entering into covenant. Basically, this is the method God chose in enacting the first covenant—the old covenant—with the children of Israel. An innocent lamb without spot, blemish, or defect was slaughtered, its blood sprinkled on the altar to atone for or cleanse the sin of the people, and its carcass burned on the altar. This was a type and a shadow of a greater sacrifice to come—a foreshadowing of when Jesus Christ, the Lamb of God, would spill His precious and sinless blood to atone for the sins of the world.

Covenant Partners

The distinguishing characteristic of both the old and new covenants in the Bible is their completely gracious and effective character due to the wholly righteous nature of God. Unlike covenants between men or nations, which are entered into by mutual agreement and negotiation, God's covenant is unilateral. He initiated it and established its terms with no input from us. Then He presented His covenant to us and invited us to enter into it with Him.

This unilateral quality to God's covenant is borne out in the meaning both of the Hebrew word *beriyth* and its Greek equivalent in the New Testament: *diatheke*. The word *diatheke*, in fact, refers to "a will that distributes one's property after death according to the owner's wishes" and as such is "completely unilateral."[6] Human covenants entail mutual requirements of aid and support from both parties. God is sovereign and omnipotent; He needs nothing from us, and there is nothing we can truly provide to Him. He provides everything in the covenant He makes with us. All He requires of us is our obedience and faithfulness.

When we enter into covenant with God, we become partners with Him—not equal partners, but partners by His grace. The only covenant God recognizes is a blood covenant. We cannot underestimate the importance of blood to our covenant partnership with the Lord. In the 9th chapter of Genesis, God says to Noah:

> *Every moving thing that lives shall be food for you.*
> *I have given you all things, even as the green herbs.*
> *But you shall not eat flesh with its life, that is, its*
> *blood"* (Genesis 9:3-4).

Much later, in Leviticus, the Lord says:

---

6.   W. E. Vine, Merrill F. Unger, and William White, Jr., *Vine's Complete Expository Dictionary of Old and New Testament Words.* (Nashville: Thomas Nelson Publishers, 1996), Old Testament Section, p. 51.

And whatever man of the house of Israel, or of the strangers who dwell among you, who eats any blood, I will set My face against that person who eats blood, and will cut him off from among his people. For the life of the flesh is in the blood, and I have given it to you upon the altar to make atonement for your souls; for it is the blood that makes atonement for the soul" (Leviticus 17:10-11).

Life is in the blood. For this reason, God commanded the Israelites never to eat it. Before they could eat their meat, they had to drain the blood and roast the meat thoroughly.

When the blood of a sacrifice is spilled, the life in the blood makes atonement. So the blood has awesome meaning; it is the very life of a person. A blood covenant involves the co-mingling of lives so that two lives become one. If you and I enter into a blood covenant, we become covenant partners. I now stand accountable for you, and you stand accountable for me. Your life is my life, and my life is your life. Our lives are blended because we have come together in the blood.

Therefore, if someone comes against you, they come against me. Likewise, an attack on me is an attack on you. I have sworn to protect you, and you have sworn to protect me. We have pledged our lives to each other.

Stop and think for a moment. What is your life? It is your family, your time, and your treasure; all your possessions, all your finances. Everything you are and have is, in a sense, wrapped up in your blood. If you lose your blood, you lose your life. When we enter into a blood covenant together, I regard your life—your family, time, treasure, resources—as though they were my own, and you do the same for me.

That is covenant, and it is a concept poorly understood today, particularly in the West. Few people today truly comprehend the depth of commitment involved in a covenant. In our modern society we tend to shy away from commitment because we don't want to be tied down. Besides, in the eyes of many, to talk about blood this way seems downright barbaric. Blood was very important to the Hebrew mind, however, because it was very important to the Hebrew God. It remains so today, despite what society says. Without blood there is no covenant.

Under a covenant, each partner's name belongs to the other. That is why as Christians we can say that we bear the name of Christ. He is ours, and we are His. Because we are under covenant and bear His name, all His resources are ours. The Lord is very generous with His resources, and because He is generous, we can be generous also.

Bonnie and I both grew up in generous families. Her parents were very generous people, and she learned that quality from them. I learned generosity from my mother, who learned it growing up in the royal houses of India. My mother was one of the most generous people I ever knew. Whenever someone visited our home, she always saw to it that they left with a gift of some kind: gold earrings or a gold chain for a woman, perhaps, or a gold pen for a gentleman. That is the way she was raised.

Our checkbook has both our names on it, and Bonnie is always writing checks to give to people who have a need or simply as a gift. Many times I don't even know anything about it until I receive a note saying something like, "Thank you so much for your generous gift of such-and-such for our so-and-so." Then I say to Bonnie, "What's this all about?"

"Oh," she laughs, "that's seed money."

"Well, do you want my shirt too?"

The point I'm making is that covenant partnership unlocks resources. As Christians, we bear the name of Jesus. Our debts are His debts, and He paid them on the cross. His interests and priorities are ours as well because we are in covenant with Him. We have a blood covenant with the living God to go into all the world and preach good news to all creation. What is the good news? It is the news that Jesus has made covenant with us so that whoever believes on Him will not perish but have eternal life.

Consider for a moment what being in covenant with the Lord means for you. On the cross, Jesus mingled His blood with yours. You shook hands with God, and God shook hands with you. His assets are now your assets. What did you have before you shook hands with Jesus? Nothing! Talk about a "rags to riches" story! Here is Jesus Christ, the Prince of Heaven, who owns the entire universe and everything in it, and now He shakes hands with you and says, "It's yours." That's what Paul means when he says that we are "joint-heirs" with Jesus (see Romans 8:17). He is our Elder Brother, our "blood brother."

Blood Brothers of Jesus

What made Jesus do it anyway? What made Him go to the cross? The answer is very simple: love. Because of love, God sent His Son to die for us. Because of love, Jesus willingly suffered death on the cross, taking our sin upon Himself that we might be redeemed. He became sin for us so that we could become the righteousness of God in Him. Because of love, Jesus spilled His blood so we could be healed.

When our son Ben was a baby and dying from kidney failure, because of the blood covenant, Jesus took the curse.

Essentially, Jesus bore Ben's disease 2,000 years ago and nailed it to the cross. Because of the blood covenant, an exchange took place. Jesus took Ben's diseased and dead kidneys and gave His own to Ben. Ben's kidneys were literally recreated. The X-rays had clearly shown that Ben's kidneys were dead. Suddenly, new X-rays showed healthy kidneys, and the doctors wanted to know what happened. Basically, I feel like I could put it this way: he got Jesus' kidneys, and Jesus took Ben's messed up kidneys on Calvary. There was an exchange.

In John 15:13 Jesus says, "Greater love has no one than this, than to lay down one's life for his friends." Because of the blood covenant, an exchange takes place. Jesus takes our death and gives us His life in its place. There is no way we can explain this; we simply have to trust and believe.

If you have been born again, you are a blood brother to Jesus Christ. You have, in a sense, taken your wrists, placed them against His bloody, nail-pierced wrists, and entered a blood covenant with Him. That means that you have committed yourself to love Him, follow Him, obey Him, and live for His interests and purposes alone. He has already demonstrated that He loves you and has your best interests at heart by dying on the cross for you and giving you access through His Spirit to all the resources that are His.

There is another dimension to this blood brotherhood. If you are a blood brother to Jesus, that means you are also a blood brother to every other person who claims the name of Christ. Fellow believers, whether they are in your church or anywhere else, are more than just friends; they are your blood brothers, and you are theirs.

This is a very holy and special relationship that we so often take much too lightly. I am convinced that if we as Western Christians would gain a better grasp of what it really means to be in covenant with one another, much of our strife, division, and infighting would simply go away. Those who understand the concept of covenant regard it as a sober undertaking with life-changing implications.

Generally speaking, Muslims understand and practice this better than many Christians. In the Muslim world, honor is of extreme importance. This is one reason why we rarely see or hear a Muslim criticizing the words or actions of another Muslim. They honor the old traditions of the covenant. If you were to enter a Muslim home and say, "I receive the hospitality of this house," you would be safe from harm as long as you remained under their roof. Even if they considered you their enemy, for the sake of the age-old concept of covenant, they would be honor-bound to afford you hospitality and protection.

Why can't we as Christians learn to treat each other that way? So many times I have seen fellowship in churches disrupted by arguments over doctrine, or worship style, or music style, or financial decisions. I have seen personal disagreements between Christians blow up into anger and resentment that lasts for years.

There are many reasons for this, not the least of which is spiritual warfare, as satan sets his sights on sowing disruption and discord among believers. I am convinced that part of the problem, however, stems from the fact that so few of us truly understand the concept of being in covenant with Christ and with each other, and all that it implies.

Once we become blood brothers and blood sisters, the covenants of God require that we act like blood brothers and blood sisters. That means loving one another, serving one another, praying for one another, never speaking evil of one another, always seeking one another's good, always seeking to build up one another, encouraging one another in the faith, and appreciating one another's gifts and unique contributions to the Body of Christ. We belong to each other just as we each belong to Christ. We have the same Father and the same destiny, and we should reflect that in the way we treat each other.

When Christians are quick to say any nasty things about each other, it is a sad commentary on our lack of understanding of what it means as the people of God to be blood brothers in Christ. As James says, "So then, my beloved brethren, let every man be swift to hear, slow to speak, slow to wrath; for the wrath of man does not produce the righteousness of God" (James 1:19-20).

I would rather die than break my covenant with Jesus. Before I knew Him, I had absolutely nothing, but now He has blessed me in ways far too numerous to count. He has healed my sons and daughters. I owe everything to Him. He is my blood brother, and I will never break faith with Him.

There is deep meaning to being a blood brother of Jesus. A blood covenant carries a code of speech and behavior all its own. Being in covenant means being part of a household of faith, and being absolutely faithful and loyal to those who are in covenant with us. It means being willing to pay the price, willing to lay down our lives for each other as Jesus laid down His life for us. Remember Jesus' words, "Greater love has no one than this, than to lay down one's life for his friends" (John 15:13).

Keeping covenant means placing others' good and welfare above our own and living a lifestyle of holiness and self-giving service. Paul wrote to the Philippians, "Let nothing be done through selfish ambition or conceit, but in lowliness of mind let each esteem others better than himself. Let each of you look out not only for his own interests, but also for the interests of others" (Philippians 2:3-4).

We are partakers of a new covenant in the blood of Jesus, and just as Christ has ministered that covenant to us, He has called us to minister it to others: "Our sufficiency is from God, who also made us sufficient as ministers of the new covenant, not of the letter but of the Spirit; for the letter kills, but the Spirit gives life" (2 Corinthians 3:5b-6). As ministers of the blood covenant, we are ministers of life, because there is life in the blood of Jesus—life and power and blessings.

Chapter Six

BLESSINGS OF THE BLOOD COVENANT

We in America have been richly blessed by God in our natural resources, in our republican form of government, and in our free society. Because we are a republic, we have no monarchy, and, therefore, no real concept of what it is like to live under a king. In some ways this is good, because we enjoy more individual freedom. One drawback for American Christians, however, is that being raised in the tradition of independence and self-reliance can make it harder for us to understand how to relate to Jesus Christ as King of kings and Lord of lords.

With our American system of checks and balances and separation of powers, we do not know what it is like to live under someone who holds absolute sovereignty. If we are dissatisfied with our leaders, we can throw them out of office on election day. Kings are different. They come to power through family line succession and generally reign for life. When we become born again, we have to learn to make a mental adjustment in order to submit ourselves to live under the absolute sovereignty of Christ as King of kings.

My mother was a very generous woman, and she learned her generosity from being raised in the royal houses of India.

Traditionally, monarchs are surrounded by so much wealth that they naturally become givers. Persons seeking an audience with the king would go away with not only their petition granted, but also a token of the king's generosity: an emerald or a ruby or a pearl, or perhaps even a diamond. My mother witnessed this all the time among the rulers in India, and generosity became part of her nature.

If earthly monarchs can be so generous in the sharing of their wealth, should we not expect our Heavenly Father, the King of the universe, to be even more generous? Jesus made this point when He said, "If you then, being evil, know how to give good gifts to your children, how much more will your Father who is in heaven give good things to those who ask Him!" (Matthew 7:11) As a benevolent King, our Lord pours out abundant gifts and blessings on all who are His under the blood covenant.

The Exceeding Riches of His Grace

By far the greatest blessing we have received from the Lord is His saving grace. Without it, we would remain forever lost and without hope. In his letter to the Ephesians, Paul eloquently describes what God's grace has done for us:

> *But God, who is rich in mercy, because of His great love with which He loved us, even when we were dead in trespasses, made us alive together with Christ (by grace you have been saved), and raised us up together, and made us sit together in the heavenly places in Christ Jesus, that in the ages to come He might show the exceeding riches of His grace in His kindness toward us in Christ Jesus. For by grace you have been saved through faith, and that not of*

*yourselves; it is the gift of God, not of works, lest
anyone should boast* (Ephesians 2:4-9).

Even when we were dead in our trespasses and sins, God
"made us alive together with Christ." He did not wait for or
demand that we change our lifestyle or "turn over a new leaf"
before He sent Jesus to die for us. He did this for us because
of His grace. The grace of God is His unmerited favor extend-
ed to us. In other words, God gives us His favor not because
we deserve it but because we need it. When we deserved judgment, He showed us mercy. What we could not do for ourselves because of our sin, God did for us—He saved us by His
grace.

God's grace becomes effective in our lives when we exercise faith in Christ, but even our faith is a gift from God. By
saving us from our sin, God displays "the exceeding riches of
His grace in His kindness toward us in Christ Jesus." God's
grace is a gift, and the faith to believe is a gift. As King of the
universe, God delights to give gifts to His children.

What do you do when someone offers you a gift? You
reach out and take it. In order for a gift to become truly yours,
you must accept it. God has offered us the marvelous gift of
His grace, but we must accept it before it will do us any good.
So often we feel unworthy of receiving anything from God.
Once we understand the depth of our own sinfulness, we may
feel like the tax collector in Jesus' parable in Luke 18:10-14,
who would not even raise his eyes toward heaven, but simply
cried out, "God, be merciful to me, a sinner!"

God is merciful to us. He is the King of kings and
extends to us not the justice we deserve, but the mercy we
need. When you are around a king, you try not to say or do
something foolish, especially if you are one of his subjects. If

he is being gracious to you and offers you a gift, you don't stand there protesting, saying, "No, no, I can't accept that. I'm not worthy." That may be how you feel, but instead of refusing, you accept the king's gift and say, "Thank you, your Majesty."

The grace of God is a gift none of us deserve but which He gives freely. Our salvation—our righteousness or right standing with God—is the result of His gift of grace, "not of works lest anyone should boast." That means we could never be "good enough" to become right with God on our own. No amount of good deeds or rule-keeping could ever earn us favor with God. He offers it freely, and it is ours for the receiving. We can get it no other way.

God's grace toward us serves a purpose beyond simply saving us. Continuing on, Paul says to the Ephesians:

> *For we are His workmanship, created in Christ Jesus for good works, which God prepared beforehand that we should walk in them. Therefore remember that you, once Gentiles in the flesh—who are called Uncircumcision by what is called the Circumcision made in the flesh by hands—that at that time you were without Christ, being aliens from the commonwealth of Israel and strangers from the covenants of promise, having no hope and without God in the world* (Ephesians 2:10-12).

Once we come to Christ, we begin to learn who we really are. God "created [us] in Christ Jesus" so that we could "walk" in "good works." We do good works *because* we are saved. As people redeemed from sin by the blood of Jesus, we have a great destiny and a great purpose. Part of that destiny is to spend our lives doing "good works" in Jesus' name.

Another part of our destiny is to spend eternity in the presence and fellowship of our Lord, who has been preparing a place for us for 2,000 years.

Without Christ, we were lost in the wilderness. There is nothing more tragic than to die without knowing the Lord, because then all hope is gone. One of the hardest things for me to do, especially after many years as a pastor and an evangelist, is to attend or conduct a funeral for someone I know was not a believer. What can you say about someone in that situation? Just about the only thing you can do is minister to the family members who are left behind. That is why it is so important for us who know the Lord to proclaim the good news of His saving grace to the world.

Brought Near by the Blood of Christ

In the verses that follow, Paul continues to describe some of the blessings we have received because we are partners in the blood covenant in Christ:

> But now in Christ Jesus you who once were far off have been brought near by the blood of Christ. For He Himself is our peace, who has made both one, and has broken down the middle wall of separation, having abolished in His flesh the enmity, that is, the law of commandments contained in ordinances, so as to create in Himself one new man from the two, thus making peace, and that He might reconcile them both to God in one body through the cross, thereby putting to death the enmity. And He came and preached peace to you who were afar off and to those who were near. For through Him we both

have access by one Spirit to the Father (Ephesians 2:13-18).

Once we were far away from God, separated from Him by our sin, but now the blood of Christ has brought us near. His blood cleansed our sin and in Christ we now have full access to the Father and to all the riches and glory of His kingdom. Christ Himself is our peace. He does not simply give us peace. Jesus comes to dwell in our hearts through His Spirit and brings peace with Him because He is peace.

Jesus brings us complete peace. In Hebrew, the word for "peace" is *shalom,* which includes in its meaning such ideas as being safe, well, happy, prosperous, and complete. In Ephesians 2:14, Paul uses the Greek word *eirene,* which refers to peace in the sense of quietness, rest, and "to set at one again." In other words, when we give our lives to Christ, He comes into our hearts and sets us at one with ourselves again. He ends the internal conflict that divides our minds.

Three times in these verses Paul uses the word "both," referring to the Gentiles and the Jews. Through His death, Jesus broke down the "wall of separation" between Jews and Gentiles, putting an end to the enmity between them. Now, all of us together are reconciled to God "through the cross" (or by the blood) of Christ. This means that through Christ we "have access by one Spirit to the Father."

The blood of Christ has brought us near the Father. As Paul explains, in Christ our status has changed from that of aliens to citizens of the kingdom of God:

Now, therefore, you are no longer strangers and foreigners, but fellow citizens with the saints and members of the household of God, having been built

on the foundation of the apostles and prophets,
Jesus Christ Himself being the chief corner stone, in
whom the whole building, being joined fitted togeth-
er, grows into a holy temple in the Lord, in whom you
also are being built together for a dwelling place of
God in the Spirit (Ephesians 2:19-22).

Not only are we citizens of God's kingdom, but we are also members of His family, His "household." Every house needs a solid foundation, which in this case is, the apostles and prophets of the early church. A cornerstone was used to bind walls together and give them added strength. The Bible uses the word "cornerstone" frequently as a symbol of strength and prominence. In the household of God, Jesus Christ Himself is the "chief cornerstone." Every individual believer comprises another "stone" added to the structure of the "holy temple in the Lord" that the Spirit is building up as a "dwelling place of God."

A Habitation of the Spirit

One of the greatest blessings we receive from the blood covenant with Jesus is that He builds us into habitations for the Spirit of God, both as individual believers and collectively as the church. Just imagine, the Spirit of the living God dwells in us! He who is too great for the universe to contain nevertheless abides with us as a continuing presence! It is a concept almost beyond human comprehension.

The devil hates the whole idea. Nothing reveals his defeat more clearly than Spirit-filled believers. That is why we are targets for his attacks. Satan moves against anyone or any place where God seeks to dwell. Therefore we must be careful to guard His habitation jealously, whether our individual lives or our collective lives as the church of the Lord Jesus Christ.

If we allow enmity, strife, jealousy, unbridled anger, evil speaking, or other sins of the flesh to gain control, we will grieve the Spirit and He will depart, leaving us desolate. This does not mean that He no longer dwells in our hearts, but that our fellowship with Him is broken. Without the Spirit of God in active control of our lives, we open ourselves up to all kinds of worldly, fleshly, sinful, and demonic influences.

When you and I came to Christ, God breathed His breath of life, His *pneuma*, His Holy Spirit into us and we became alive in Christ. When we come together with other believers in a local church fellowship, the Lord breathes His life and power through us as a corporate body, the Body of Christ.

It is so tragic, therefore, to see so many individual believers and churches who will not allow themselves to be habitations of God's Spirit because they deny many of the things of the Spirit. "Oh, the Spirit is okay," they say, "but we don't want any of that lifting of hands, or speaking in tongues, or prophecy. We don't accept any of that stuff."

What they are really saying is they won't accept a Holy Spirit they cannot control. The Spirit is okay as long as He doesn't do anything "weird" or unexpected. As long as they can keep the Spirit safely in a theological box of their own design, they're fine. Attempting to restrict the Spirit of God in this manner amounts to rejecting Him. God's Spirit will not be controlled by human will or opinion. Where He is not welcomed, He simply departs.

Except for outer space, nothing survives long in a vacuum. If the departure of one thing creates a vacuum, something else will come along quickly to fill it. This is especially true in the spiritual realm. Either we are filled with the Spirit of God, or we will be filled with another kind of spirit. Jesus gave a clear warning in this regard:

When an unclean spirit goes out of a man, he goes through dry places, seeking rest, and finds none. Then he says, "I will return to my house from which I came." And when he comes, he finds it empty, swept, and put in order. Then he goes and takes with him seven other spirits more wicked than himself, and they enter and dwell there; and the last state of that man is worse than the first. So shall it also be with this wicked generation (Matthew 12:43-45).

God intends for us to be habitations for His Spirit. If we reject the Holy Spirit, nothing is left except the spirit of the enemy. This is what happened in Germany in the first part of the 20th century. Church authorities in Germany rejected the great visitation of the Holy Spirit that had begun with revivals in Wales and in the Scandinavian countries. They said, "We don't want anything to do with the Holy Spirit." So the Holy Spirit stayed out of Germany. By rejecting the Holy Spirit, they opened the door for the satanic spirit to gain a foothold. This is one reason why the Nazis were able to come to power in Germany in the 1930s. The demonic power of antichrist was the driving force behind Nazism, and the German church had little with which to fight it. Rejection of the Holy Spirit had rendered them almost useless against such evil. Many German churches and leaders even bought into the Nazi party line and allied themselves with the party doctrines and agenda.

In the aftermath of the horrors that Nazi Germany unleashed on the world, many have asked in the years since, "How could human beings do such things?" Fallen, sinful human nature is capable of tremendous, almost unthinkable evil. Coupled with the influence of demonic powers, human beings can be quite hideous in their thoughts, actions, and schemes. Virtually anything is possible.

It is a matter of spiritual warfare. Either the Holy Spirit rules in our lives, or the devil will. Where the Holy Spirit has been made welcome, anti-Semitism goes away, racism goes away, and class envy, resentment, and pride go away. The Holy Spirit makes us all one in Christ and gives us all equal access to the Father and to the resources of His kingdom. As believers, we are habitations of God. Through His Spirit, God dwells in us.

If you are serious about guarding yourself as a habitation for God's Spirit, be careful to control your tongue. Uncontrolled speech such as cursing (not only profanity, but also speaking curses), gossip, negative speech, and speaking evil of elders or others in the church can do indescribable damage.

Take care also to read, study, and meditate on the Word of God, and to devote yourself regularly to prayer. Regarding prayer, don't neglect speaking in tongues, your special prayer language of the Spirit. Consider the words of Paul, "Finally, brethren, whatever things are true, whatever things are noble, whatever things are just, whatever things are pure, whatever things are lovely, whatever things are of good report, if there is any virtue and if there is anything praiseworthy—meditate on these things" (Philippians 4:8).

One Word, One Woman, One Sword

Receiving the blessings of the blood covenant is contingent upon loyalty, faithfulness, and obedience to the conditions of the covenant. It calls for oneness of mind and purpose. Fidelity to the blood covenant is similar to a principle I learned being raised in an aristocratic Indian home: *one word, one woman, one sword.*

"One word" meant that when you gave your word, you would die before breaking it. No matter the personal cost or how much trouble or hurt you might suffer as a result, you would never break your word. As Christians, our word should be our bond. No one should ever have any reason to question our honesty or integrity because we were untrue to something we said. Jesus said, "But let your 'Yes' be 'Yes,' and your 'No,' 'No.' For whatever is more than these is from the evil one" (Matthew 5:37). In other words, say what you mean, mean what you say, and follow through. Keep your word.

"One woman" meant to be true to your relationships. Marriage is a covenant: one man and one woman faithful for life. The marriage covenant is such a powerful image that the Bible uses it over and over to refer to God's relationship to His people. Israel's unfaithfulness to God by worshiping idols is described time and again as spiritual *adultery*—breaking of covenant. For covenant men and women, adultery is not only immoral, but also dishonorable. As with keeping your word, it would be better to die than to be unfaithful either to your mate or to your God.

"One sword" meant that your enemy is my enemy, and we stand together. Going into battle is a serious thing. You never fight unless you really mean it, for once you draw your sword you will not put it back without blood on it. Sometimes this part of the promise was sealed with a "blood oath," similar to cutting a blood covenant, where each person would cut or prick his arm or finger until the blood flowed as a sign of his commitment to the other. The idea was to make a potential enemy think twice before attacking. Alliances between nations serve a similar purpose. The spirit behind "one sword" was, "If you pick a fight with *them*, you have a fight with *me*." It's all about loyalty.

A Covenant Between Kings

One of the most powerful illustrations of love, loyalty, and covenant-keeping in all of Scripture is found in the relationship between David and Jonathan. The story spans parts of First and Second Samuel. Jonathan was the son of Saul, Israel's first king, and therefore natural heir to the throne of Israel. David was a shepherd who had become a renowned warrior in Israel for killing the giant Goliath and for other exploits in battle. He had also been anointed to become Israel's second king. The son of the first king meeting the man destined to become the second king sounds like a setup for conflict, but it was anything but that.

Because of Saul's disobedience, God had determined to take the kingdom away from him and give it to David. Although Saul surrendered more and more to the powers of spiritual darkness, his son Jonathan was a godly man and a great warrior.

David, for his part, was not greedy to be king. He was willing to wait for God's timing. On several occasions David had the opportunity to kill Saul and take the kingdom, but he refused to lift his hand against God's anointed. David recognized Saul as God's chosen king, and would not take matters into his own hands. It is important that even when we see our destiny, that we do not grab it impatiently, but let the Lord bring us into it. That is what David did.

Perceiving David as a threat to his throne, Saul sought to kill him. David was constantly on the run, hiding out in the caves and the mountains as the leader of a band of other fugitives. Many times they were only one short step ahead of being caught and destroyed by Saul and his army. For a long time, Jonathan was in the dark about his father's murderous intent toward David.

Even though he was the "rightful" heir to the throne as Saul's son, Jonathan recognized that God had anointed David to be king instead. The Bible says that David and Jonathan shared a love for each other that was deeper than the love between brothers, and they made a blood covenant with each other. After meeting in a field and devising a plan whereby Jonathan would determine his father's intentions and inform David, Jonathan said:

> *"The Lord God of Israel is witness! When I have sounded out my father sometime tomorrow, or the third day, and indeed there is good toward David, and I do not send to you and tell you, may the Lord do so and much more to Jonathan. But if it pleases my father to do you evil, then I will report it to you and send you away, that you may go in safety. And the Lord be with you as He has been with my father. And you shall not only show me the kindness of the Lord while I still live, that I may not die; but you shall not cut off your kindness from my house forever, no, not when the Lord has cut off every one of the enemies of David from the face of the earth." So*

Jonathan made a covenant with the house of David, saying, "Let the Lord require it at the hand of David's enemies." Now Jonathan again caused David to vow, because he loved him; for he loved him as he loved his own soul (1 Samuel 20:12-17).

Jonathan was saying to David, "I recognize you as the Israel's true king, and lay down my claim to the throne. In return, show kindness to me and protect me as long as I live, and no matter what happens to me, take care of my family."

Some time later, Saul and Jonathan were both killed while fighting the Philistines. When David heard the news, he mourned deeply, not just for Jonathan but for Saul as well. Despite all of Saul's past efforts to kill him, David had only good to say about the dead king and his son: "Saul and Jonathan were beloved and pleasant in their lives, and in their death they were not divided; they were swifter than eagles, they were stronger than lions" (2 Samuel 1:23).

Eating at the King's Table

Saul and Jonathan were dead, and David was now king, just as God planned. In ancient days when one king took over the throne from another king, it was common practice for the new king to kill the remaining members of the old king's family, particularly his sons and grandsons, to eliminate potential threats to his rule. When word of the deaths of Saul and Jonathan reached their homes, their families fled in haste, probably expecting David to seek swift retribution.

Jonathan had a five-year-old son named Mephibosheth who became crippled in his feet and legs after his nurse accidentally dropped him in her haste to get away. His existence unknown to David, Mephibosheth grew up in Lo-Debar, a city with long and well-established loyalties to Saul's family. It is quite possible that during those years Mephibosheth learned to hate and fear David and wrongfully believe him responsible for the deaths of Saul and Jonathan.

Once David's reign was solidly established, he was quick to act on his covenant promise to Jonathan:

> *Now David said, "Is there still anyone who is left of the house of Saul, that I may show him kindness for Jonathan's sake?"...And Ziba said to the king, "There is still a son of Jonathan who is lame in his feet." ...Then King David sent and brought him out of the house of Machir the son of Ammiel, from Lo Debar. Now when Mephibosheth the son of Jonathan, the son of Saul, had come to David, he fell on his face and prostrated himself, then David said, "Mephibosheth?" And he answered, "Here is your servant!" So David said to him, "Do not fear, for I will surely show you kindness for Jonathan your father's sake, and will restore to you all the land of Saul your grandfather; and you shall eat bread at my table continually"* (2 Samuel 9:1, 3b, 5-7).

To this generous gesture on the king's part, Mephibosheth replied, "What is your servant, that you should look upon such a dead dog as I?" (2 Samuel 9:8)

This may have been more than a simple expression of humility; Mephibosheth may have considered himself a "dead dog" because, as a member of Saul's family, he had expected David to kill him. Instead, he found himself in possession of the estate that had previously belonged to his grandfather, Saul. In addition, he ate at David's table every day "like one of the king's sons" (2 Samuel 9:11). There was no higher honor in the land than to eat at the king's table. Among other things, this meant that Mephibosheth never had to worry about making a living or having to fend for himself. David treated Mephibosheth with kindness and generosity for Jonathan's sake. David's blood covenant with Jonathan transcended generations.

All the Promises of God

Paul says in Ephesians 2:1 that before we came to Christ we were dead in our trespasses and sins. Like Mephibosheth, we were "dead dogs" with regard to the kingdom of God. God's desire to intervene and bless humanity caused Him to send His Son to die so that our sins could be forgiven. Jesus took our sins upon Himself—yours, mine, and everybody else's—and with His own blood "cut covenant" with us. He went before the Father and said, "My blood for their lives," and bought our redemption. Now everything that belongs to Jesus also belongs to us.

The signs of the covenant are the cuts in the hands, feet, and side of Jesus. When the Father sees those cuts, He remembers the covenant and says to us, "I will show mercy and loving kindness to you for the sake of Jesus, My Son, who sealed a blood covenant with His own blood on your behalf."

Because we are beneficiaries of the blood covenant, all the riches, promises, and blessings of God are ours. There are conditions that we must satisfy in order to enjoy the full benefits of the covenant. We must walk in obedience to the Word and the will of God, be filled with the Spirit of God, and give ourselves to be God's "workmanship" to the nations, "created in Christ Jesus for good works" (Ephesians 2:10). There is no higher privilege than to partner with God in proclaiming the good news of redemption from sin through the blood of His Son, Jesus Christ, the King of kings and Lord of lords.

All the promises and blessings of God are yours. What do you need today physically, emotionally, mentally, or spiritually? What are your family's needs? Blood covenant transcends generations. As you walk in the covenant, God blesses your children and your children's children through you. The blood covenant in Christ makes it possible for you to stand in faith and say, "Lord, I cry out for my children, my grandchildren, and my great-grandchildren, that they will all serve You, the living God."

In the fellowship of the Body of Christ we share the covenant meal, the wine and the bread, as a memorial to the One who through His blood brought us into covenant with the Father. The wine and the bread represent the new covenant in His blood, and as often as we share it, we do so in remembrance of Him.

This covenant meal also reminds us that one day we will sit at the King's table, sharing His fellowship for all eternity. In the meantime, we will face times when the devil will challenge us, saying, "Who do you think you are? After all, look at what you did! You sinned here, you failed God over there; you really blew it this time! Do you really think God cares about you anymore?"

Satan will try to make you think you are a "dead dog." He is an expert at that. Learn not to cooperate with him. When he brings up those things up, just remind him, "Yes, I did those things once, but now I am a child of the King of kings. He washed me clean in His blood and now I am under the blood covenant with Him, and will sit at His table in glory through eternal ages."

Early in his second letter the apostle Peter wrote:

Grace and peace be multiplied to you in the knowledge of God and of Jesus our Lord, as His divine power has given to us all things that pertain to life and godliness, through the knowledge of Him who called us by glory and virtue, by which have been given to us exceedingly great and precious promises, that through these you may be partakers of the divine nature, having escaped the corruption that is in the world through lust (2 Peter 1:2-4).

Under the blood covenant, all the promises of God are ours. He has given us everything we need to live holy and godly lives. Through His promises we can partake of His divine nature and be renewed in body, mind, and spirit from the corruption of sin in the world. The Lord has promised to supply all our needs through His riches in glory in Christ Jesus (see Philippians 4:19). What does it cost us in return? Nothing less than giving our lives to Him in obedience to His Word and service to others in His name. He bought us with a price and we belong to Him.

We have an awesome covenant with God, a blood covenant with the King of kings, and it is something wonderful. His privileges are for you, for me, for our families, and for everyone who will believe on His name. Faith in Christ brings us into the blessings of the blood covenant, which is made effective on the basis of His blood given for our sins.

As in Jonathan Mephibosheth was blessed, in Jesus you are blessed: "For you know the grace of our Lord Jesus Christ, that though He was rich, yet for your sakes He became poor, that you through His poverty might become rich" (2 Corinthians 8:9). "God is able to make all grace abound toward you, that you, always having all sufficiency in all things, may have an abundance for every good work" (2 Corinthians 9:8). All of this is made possible through the blood covenant, and it all belongs to you.

Chapter Seven

PLEADING THE BLOOD

Some of the most popular programs on television these days are the criminal justice series. Stories about law and order, crime and punishment, and the judicial process naturally appeal to many people because of their high drama and emotion. A crime is committed, evidence is gathered, suspects are investigated, and finally, one of those suspects is arrested and formally charged with the crime. At the arraignment, a judge asks the accused, "How do you plea?" If the accused answers, "Not guilty," the judge then sets a trial date. The prosecution begins building its case against the accused, trying to prove his or her guilt. At the same time, the defense attorney works hard to prepare a defense that will counter the prosecution's case and at the very least create reasonable doubt as to the guilt of the accused.

How do you plea? Are you guilty or not guilty? These are questions we should all ask ourselves because we have an adversary who is always accusing us, and we need to know how to answer him. Like an aggressive prosecuting attorney, satan is relentless in his accusations. He never lets up, and unless we know where our defense lies, we have no hope of defeating him.

We cannot stand on our good deeds or our good intentions, nor on the fact that we go to church, pray, read our Bibles, and give our tithe. No amount of our "goodness" is sufficient to overcome the devil's accusations or the reality of our own sinfulness. Isaiah 64:6 says, "But we are all like an unclean thing, and all our righteousnesses are like filthy rags; we all fade as a leaf, and our iniquities, like the wind, have taken us away."

Our defense—our *plea*—lies only in the blood of Jesus. His blood alone can take away our sins. His blood alone can answer the enemy's charges. Remember that we overcome our accuser "by the blood of the Lamb and by the word of [our] testimony" (Revelation 12:11). When we learn to plead the blood of Jesus, we will be able to silence all of satan's accusations against us and build a hedge of protection around ourselves, our families, our churches, and our circumstances.

Imagine the scene: you are standing before the bench in the courtroom of the Lord God Almighty, the great Judge over all the earth. On one side of you stands your adversary, the devil, flinging accusation after accusation about all your sins, mistakes, and failures. On the other side, as close to you as a brother, stands your Advocate and Counselor, the Lord Jesus Christ, the best defense attorney you could ever have.

The more the devil accuses you, the worse you feel. He talks about the times you lied, cheated, or stole, and the times you used harsh and hateful words toward your spouse or your children. He brings up all the times you let God down. He calls you worthless, no-good, and unworthy of anything other than the harshest sentence. As the charges mount, you feel a desperate desire to speak up in your own defense, but your

Advocate gently squeezes your arm as if to say, "Be patient and hold your peace."

Finally, the Judge turns His eyes on you and asks, "How do you plea?" Your Advocate replies for you, saying, "My client pleads the blood of Jesus." The Judge raps His gavel on the bench and declares, "So be it! Not guilty!"

It's that simple. The blood of Jesus—and *only* the blood of Jesus—can silence the enemy's accusations. No matter how long your "rap sheet" or how serious your offenses, the blood of Jesus can wipe your slate clean.

No Self-Defense

It has been said that he who serves as his own counsel has a fool for a client. Whenever we face off with the devil or go before God, the Righteous Judge, we should never try to defend ourselves. We *have* no self-defense. First of all, if we go against the devil in our own strength or wisdom, we will lose every time. Second, when we stand before God as sinners, we have nothing of our own to offer that is good enough to win our acquittal.

We certainly cannot plead innocence; that would be a lie. Romans 3:23 says, "For all have sinned and fall short of the glory of God." Neither can we claim our own goodness or merit as a defense. "But Lord, I am really a good person. Just look at all my good deeds. I am good to my family; I help widows and orphans; I coach Little League; I tithe at church; and I give generously to charities. I don't smoke and I don't chew and I don't hang with folks who do. I have never kicked the dog, and I have never ever cheated on my taxes!" All those things are commendable, (and they may even be true!), but if we try that line of reasoning with God, He will declare us guilty for sure. Good deeds and right living are not the basis for our righteousness and innocence before the Lord.

Instead, we would be much better off listening to our Advocate because He knows much more about our situation than we do. His counsel is, "Don't try to defend yourself. Plead the blood of Jesus; plead *My* blood. My blood will speak for you and say, 'Mercy, Father, and forgiveness, for this one is innocent.'"

If we learn to rely solely on the blood that Jesus Christ, the Lamb of God, poured out on our behalf, we will win every time. The devil can counterfeit many things, but he cannot counterfeit the blood of Jesus. He has absolutely no answer for it or defense against it. When we plead the blood of Jesus, nothing satan brings against us will stand—no lie, no slander, no accusation, no condemnation, no guilt, no shame. In every instance we overcome by the blood of the Lamb and the word of our testimony.

It is important, therefore, that we trust the Lord and commit ourselves fully to Him, placing our faith in what *He* has done for us rather than trusting in ourselves. We must not be like the seven sons of Sceva in Acts 19:13-16, who did not know the Lord but tried to exorcise demons "by the Jesus whom Paul preaches," only to be beaten up and run off by the evil spirits.

Secondhand knowledge of the Lord is not enough; we have to know Him personally. Being washed in the blood of Jesus is a *personal* experience. Through faith we must know what Christ has done for us and won for us through His death, burial, and resurrection.

How well do you know the gospel, the good news of the Lord Jesus Christ? Could you tell someone else about the healings of Jesus, His casting out of demons, or His teachings in the Sermon on the Mount? Most important of all, could you tell that person about how Jesus came to save him or her from sin, how He died on the cross, was buried, and three days later rose from the dead? *That* and that alone is the basis of our salvation.

The Blood of the Lamb: Our Protection

Many believers are confused by the expression "pleading the blood of Jesus." Even some of the folks who *use* the expression don't truly understand what it means. Let's put it in context. The *blood* of Jesus is the weapon we use against the accusations of the enemy. *Pleading* the blood is the tactic, or the manner in which we wield the weapon.

God told the Israelites in Egypt how to protect themselves against the judgment that was coming on the land. All they had to do was swab their doorposts with lamb's blood. In the natural, that seemed an unlikely protection. The spiritual realm, however, operates on different principles from the physical. Once the Israelites were "under the blood," the destroyer could not touch them. The Egyptians had no such protection, and millions of their firstborn died that night.

Like those ancient Egyptians, we all have a divine appointment before the judgment seat of God. As with the Israelites, however, protection is available to us. Someone said that just as the safest place to be in the midst of a raging forest fire is where the fire has already burned, the safest place to be at the judgment is at the cross, where judgment has already passed. When we place ourselves "under the blood" of Jesus at the cross, satan's accusations lose their force and power. The sentence of condemnation is lifted from our heads. Jesus bore it away and set us free. Our "Egypt" of sin and bondage lies behind us and our "promised land" of grace, peace, health, prosperity, and redemption stretches before us.

We need to learn how to aggressively plead the blood of Jesus in intercession over our families, our children and grandchildren, our churches, our leaders, the people of our nation and, indeed, of all nations. These are dangerous times in which we live, and our enemy is hard at work. Satan and his minions have always been busy, but over the last century we have witnessed new levels of evil never seen before. The spirit of antichrist is loose in the world.

Here are just a few examples. The Nazis under Hitler annihilated 6 million European Jews and plunged the world into its worst war in history. As dictator of the Soviet Union, Joseph Stalin carried out multiple "purges" in which he murdered millions of his own people. During his nine years in power, Idi Amin, the "Butcher of Uganda," killed as many as 500,000 people in his country, including thousands upon thousands of Christians. Images and reports coming from Iraq in the wake of the recent war have revealed to the world much more than was previously known of the full extent of Saddam Hussein's repression, brutalization, and terrorization of the Iraqi people. More Christians were martyred for their faith during the 20th century than during all previous centuries *combined*.

International terrorism has been a growing problem for decades, but has accelerated dramatically since the 1970s. The terrorist attacks on the World Trade Center and the Pentagon on September 11, 2001 brought the shock, the horror, and the fear—as well as a new sense of vulnerability—close to home for all Americans.

It is not just us, however. In 1998, terrorists blew up the U. S. embassy in Nairobi, Kenya, killing 291 and wounding over 5,000. Most of the dead and wounded were Kenyans. Five years later, in November, 2002, another terrorist attack in Kenya destroyed the Paradise, an Israeli-owned hotel in the coastal city of Mombasa. Fifteen people were killed and scores injured. Once again, most of the victims were Kenyan.

I was raised in Mombasa many years ago. It is a beautiful city, and I had many friends within several of the various tribes. Most of the tribes are poor, and one tribe in particular that I remember loved to sing and dance while playing home-made drums. On the day of the terrorist attack, a group of performers from this tribe had gone into Mombasa to welcome Israeli visitors to the Paradise hotel. They didn't earn much, perhaps a quarter a day, but they loved to sing and dance and play their drums. It was during their performance that the terrorists struck. Many of the dead were from this performing group who had simply come to the city to welcome the tourists.

The terrorists responsible for these acts are a vicious, hate-filled enemy driven by a fanatic and deluded devotion to a false religion. They are the enemy of all decent people in the world. Lest we lose our perspective, however, we need to remember that they are inspired by the greatest enemy of all: satan and all his evil principalities. These people need not our hatred, our anger, or even our pity; they need our *prayers* and our *intercession*. The same Christ who set us free with His blood can also set them free, and He wants to.

As followers of Christ, we have the responsibility and the calling from the Lord to plead the blood of Jesus for ourselves, our families, our households, our cities, and wherever we go. The church of Jesus Christ has been given a mighty weapon that can not only protect us but also bring down the strongholds and kingdom of the enemy, and we must learn to wield it with boldness and confidence. Our Lord has given us the commission and the authority to do so.

With the hazards of life in the modern world, we certainly should be thankful for the soldiers, sailors, marines, airmen, police, and others who put their lives on the line to protect our life and liberty on a daily basis. At the same time, we must never forget that our primary weapon in the struggle is the blood of the Lamb, Jesus Christ. When we plead the blood of Jesus, we can cover and protect our spouses, our children, our friends, our neighbors, our church family, our spiritual leaders, our civic leaders—everyone.

The blood of Jesus is our protection, but we need to apply it. The lamb's blood afforded the Israelites no protection until they applied it to their doorposts. Likewise, we must apply Jesus' blood to the "doorposts" of our lives. This means coming together—praying, interceding, working, being faithful at home and at church, loving the Lord and each other, and never giving up. For the blood of Jesus to be effective, we must combine action with belief. We overcome by the blood of the Lamb *and* the word of our testimony. Our testimony is more than spoken words; it is the witness of our daily lives. The blood of Jesus is powerful, and we overcome by living according to what we say we believe. Belief plus action will protect us and give us the victory.

Don't Walk Away from the Blood Line

Pleading the blood opens up a whole dimension of fullness and richness in the provision of God that most of us have never imagined. Psalm 105:37 says, "He also brought them out with silver and gold, and there was none feeble among His tribes." The verse refers to the exodus, when the children of Israel left Egypt with "silver and gold"—the spoils of the Egyptians—and went out with no sicknesses or infirmities of any kind. The Lord healed them all.

God brought them out with silver and gold, and there were none feeble among them. When we become one with the Word of God through the blood of Jesus, this same privilege is ours. If the enemy tries to attack your health, you can line yourself up with the Word of God and say, "There are none feeble in our midst." Plead the blood for your back or your leg, or your wife's headaches or your son's arm, or whatever the problem may be. Claim the Word of God: "Lord, You said, 'There are none feeble in your midst.' I pray right now for my husband. Heal my children. Let there be none feeble in our midst."

If the enemy attacks one of your children physically or emotionally, are you going to just sit back and let it happen, or are you going to fight? Whether we like it or not, we are in a war with an implacable enemy who is tireless and never gives up. We have to be ready to fight for our children, our homes, our blessings, our health, our finances; anything that is important in our lives can become a target. Pleading the blood releases a spiritual cover that protects and delivers us. It is not a magical formula, but an exercise of faith. The blood of Jesus is powerful, but the devil is relentless, and we must be aggressive in our faith. Against the combined might of the blood of Jesus and the word of our testimony, satan's assault will collapse.

If the blood of a lamb was able to deliver a nation of several million people out of slavery overnight, just think how much more Jesus Christ, our Passover Lamb can do in saving us, delivering us, healing us, and providing for us. "For indeed Christ, our Passover, was sacrificed for us" (1 Corinthians 5:7b).

As new covenant believers, we have every right to draw a faith blood line that the devil cannot cross. By speaking words of faith, we apply the blood over the doorposts of our lives and on the outer edges of everything that belongs to us. However far your sphere of authority or blessing extends, apply the blood. No matter what, don't leave the protection the blood provides.

Some believers seem to think they can prance around any time, drop in and out of church, say nasty things about their pastor or fellow church members, go off in a huff, or just wander around doing whatever they feel like doing. They don't realize how close to the fire they are dancing or that they may get burned pretty soon. The Bible says that God is not mocked and that whatever we sow we will reap. Anytime we walk away from foundational truths, we're headed for trouble. Don't expect the blessings and protection of the blood covenant if you are not faithfully living according to the blood covenant. The children of Israel thought they could, and it led to disaster. Stay the course. Keep the faith. As you honor God, He will honor you and bless you and cause all that you do to prosper. Don't *ever* walk away from the blood line.

The Scarlet Cord of Salvation

Our God is merciful, just, and loving. It is not His desire that anyone perish and go to hell. He would much rather bless than curse, save than condemn, and justify than judge.

Even in the midst of judgment, God always extends the opportunity for deliverance for anyone who will repent and believe.

One of the best examples of this in all of Scripture involves a woman named Rahab. Her story is so significant that the writer of Hebrews mentions her in the "roll call of the faithful" in chapter 11. It is only a brief statement, but enough to relate what happened:

> *By faith the walls of Jericho fell down after they were encircled for seven days. By faith the harlot Rahab did not perish with those who did not believe, when she had received the spies with peace* (Hebrews 11:30-31).

Rahab was not born into the community of Israel, nor was she a blood descendant of Abraham. She was a harlot from the city of Jericho, a city and people so wicked in their lifestyle and pagan practices that God had commanded that they be utterly destroyed by the Israelites as judgment. Such a pronouncement may seem harsh by our standards of thinking, but God knew that the evil in Jericho was too deeply seated to be rooted out. Judgment by total destruction was the only answer. Yet, even in the midst of impending disaster, a way of escape was available, and Rahab took advantage of it.

Shortly before the Israelites crossed the Jordan River and entered the land of Canaan, Joshua dispatched two spies to scope out the land, and especially Jericho. The spies found lodging at Rahab's house. When word got out that Israelite spies were in the city, Rahab hid the men under stalks of flax on her roof. In helping them escape, Rahab asked for their protection:

> *I know that the Lord has given you the land, that the terror of you has fallen on us, and that all the*

inhabitants of the land are fainthearted because of you....The Lord your God, He is God in heaven above and on earth beneath. Now therefore, I beg you, swear to me by the Lord, since I have shown you kindness, that you also will show kindness to my father's house, and give me a true token, and spare my father, my mother, my brothers, my sisters, and all that they have, and deliver our lives from death (Joshua 2:9, 11b, 12-13).

Rahab had come to the conclusion that the God of Israel was the one true God. Expressing her faith to the two spies, she cast her lot with Israel, pleading for her sake and on behalf of her family to come under their protection. Israel as a nation was under the blood covenant, and by seeking asylum for herself and her family, Rahab was in effect pleading the blood. She was asking for acceptance into that same blood covenant.

The Israelite spies gave Rahab the answer she was hoping for:

So the men answered her, "Our lives for yours, if none of you tell this business of ours. And it shall be, when the Lord has given us the land, that we will deal kindly and truly with you....We will be blameless of this oath of yours which you have made us swear, unless, when we come into the land, you bind this line of scarlet cord in the window through which you let us down, and unless you bring your father, your mother, your brothers, and all your father's household to your own home. So it shall be that whoever goes outside the doors of your house into the street, his blood shall be on his own head, and we will be guiltless. And whoever is with you in

the house, his blood shall be on our head if a hand
is laid on him (Joshua 2:14, 17-19).

Rahab had asked for a token or a sign that she and her family would be protected. The two spies told her to tie a scarlet cord in the window of her house that overlooked the city wall—the same window they were using to escape from the city. This scarlet cord symbolized Rahab's faith in God's provision of blood under the old covenant. She made sure that the symbol of that blood was tied securely because her life depended on it, as well as the lives of her family. It was her scarlet cord of salvation.

By the time the Israelites invaded Jericho, Rahab had gathered all her family members under her roof. Although the rest of the city and its inhabitants were destroyed, Rahab and her family found protection and salvation under the blood:

And the young men who had been spies went in and
brought out Rahab, her father, her mother, her
brothers, and all that she had. So they brought out
all her relatives and left them outside the camp of
Israel....And Joshua spared Rahab the harlot, her
father's household, and all that she had. So she
dwells in Israel to this day, because she hid the mes-
sengers whom Joshua sent to spy out Jericho
(Joshua 6:23, 25).

Because of her faith in the Lord, Rahab was spared along with her family and all their possessions. Eventually, she became part of the ancestral line of Jesus Christ Himself. Jesus was of the line of King David, and Rahab was David's great-, great- grandmother. The Lord can redeem any situation. Because of the blood covenant, one who was under the judgment of total destruction was spared and became part of the line that brought the Lamb of God, the Savior of mankind, into the world. Pleading the blood is powerful; it can change our destiny and alter history.

Redeemed by the Blood of the Lamb

D o you want spiritual protection in the day to day conflicts of life? Get into the habit of pleading the blood of Jesus every day over your home, your children, their school, your finances—every aspect of life. As believers, our souls are forever secure in Christ, but we need to stay alert to the challenges and dangers that wait at every turn. There are all kinds of negative or evil influences, philosophies, and spiritual forces at work around us: political correctness, humanism, communism, erosion of moral standards, sexual perversion, denial of God, drugs, alcohol, religious cults and other false religions—you name it. We must be ever on our guard or at some point satan will trip us up and we will fall down.

When pleading the blood, we would do good to let Rahab be our pattern and example. She pleaded for her parents, her children, her brothers and sisters—everyone who was important to her. We should do the same, regularly and aggressively. Now is not the time for half-measures. If a harlot, who had no covenant with God, received by faith God's protection for herself, her family, and her possessions, how much more we as believers in Christ and partakers of the blood covenant with Him should be able to do with our faith!

Jesus Christ has redeemed us by His blood, and that redemption can extend to everything and everyone within our sphere of influence. Simon Peter wrote, "You were not redeemed with corruptible things, like silver or gold, from your aimless conduct received by tradition from your fathers, but with the precious blood of Christ, as of a lamb without blemish and without spot" (1 Peter 1:18-19).

Likewise, Paul told the Colossians, "He has delivered us from the power of darkness and conveyed us into the kingdom of the Son of His love, in whom we have redemption through His blood, the forgiveness of sins" (Colossians 1:13-14).

We are redeemed by the blood of the Lamb. As Psalm 107:2 challenges us, "Let the redeemed of the Lord say so, whom He has redeemed from the hand of the enemy." Not only should we be busy pleading the blood, but we should be happy to proclaim the Lord's redemption wherever we go. The old gospel hymn captures this thought so well:

Redeemed how I love to proclaim it!
Redeemed by the blood of the Lamb;
Redeemed through His infinite mercy,
His child, and forever I am.

There are different ways of speaking when pleading the blood. Remember that this is no magic formula, but the application by faith of a spiritual principle. Someone might say simply, "I apply the blood of Jesus to this situation." Another might say, "I sprinkle the blood of Jesus on my home." Still someone else might proclaim, "I resist the evil one with the blood of the Lamb."

Another way is by figuratively drawing a blood line that the devil cannot cross. Draw a blood line around your property. If you are a businessperson or other professional, draw a blood line around your business or practice. If you are a teacher, draw a blood line around your school and around your classroom. If you are a plumber or an electrician, you might want to draw a blood line around your truck. By drawing a blood line you can cover your home, your business, your family, and your possessions and protect them from the evil one. You can say, "I apply the blood of Jesus to this situation," and bind the enemy's power.

There is power in the blood of Jesus that sets everything right, and His blood is working in us now to defeat every evil work. First Peter 5:8-9 says, "Be sober, be vigilant; because your adversary the devil walks about like a roaring lion, seeking whom he may devour. Resist him, steadfast in the faith, knowing that the same sufferings are experienced by your brotherhood in the world." The more we learn to stand fast in faith under the covering of Jesus' blood, the more we will overcome the attacks and accusations of the enemy.

This is a time of war, and it is imperative that we stand fast and cry out for the protection of the blood of Jesus for our households, for our children wherever they are, for our armed forces, our government leaders, and our brothers and sisters in Christ. The blood can keep us safe in perilous times.

There is a speaking power in the blood of Jesus. Hebrews 12:24 refers to "the blood of sprinkling that speaks better things than that of Abel." The blood testifies that Jesus has set us free from every curse and made us partakers in the inheritance of the saints. God worked when the blood of Abel cried to Him. How much more mightily will He work when the blood of Jesus, His own Son, cries out to Him!

By pleading the blood, we agree with what the blood says concerning our total and absolute redemption and freedom from the curse. We overcome our accuser by the blood of the Lamb and the word of our testimony, and therefore total victory is ours. Paul said, "The weapons of our warfare are not

carnal but mighty in God for pulling down strongholds"
(2 Corinthians 10:4).

Some of those weapons are the name of Jesus, the Word
of God, and the precious blood of the Lamb. With such an
arsenal at our disposal, we cannot help but overcome. There is
power in the blood of Jesus: power to overcome every challenge and every adversary, and power to achieve complete and
total victory in Jesus' name.

Chapter Eight

WARFARE IN THE POWER OF THE BLOOD

G od has revealed Himself through His Word, first
through His written Word, the Bible, and finally through
His incarnate Word, His Son, Jesus Christ. There is no other
revelation. No matter what form it takes, God's Word is living
and dynamic, able to impact our lives and change the course
of history. Concerning the written Word, the writer of Hebrews
says:

> *The Word of God is living and powerful, and sharp-*
> *er than any two-edged sword, piercing even to the*
> *division of soul and spirit, and of joints and mar-*
> *row, and is a discerner of the thoughts and intents*
> *of the heart* (Hebrews 4:12).

The Bible is no dry and lifeless treatise on theology and
doctrine. It contains both, but in its essence it is the dynamic
expression of the heart of the living God.

With regard to Jesus Christ, the incarnate Word, the apostle John had this to say:

> *In the beginning was the Word, and the Word was*
> *with God, and the Word was God. He was in the*
> *beginning with God...And the Word became flesh*

and dwelt among us, and we beheld His glory, the glory as of the only begotten of the Father, full of grace and truth (John 1:1-2,14).

Jesus Christ is the ultimate and final revelation of God. All we need to know about God we can learn by looking at Jesus, for when we see Him we see the Father; when we know Jesus we know the Father. Of course, God also gives us signs, wonders, and miracles, but these do not constitute new revelation. They merely accompany and confirm the revelation God has already given in His Word.

When you come right down to it, knowing the Lord is all the knowledge we really need. Don't get me wrong; I have nothing against academic study and scholarship. Intellectual knowledge is important and beneficial, particularly when pursued within the context of faith and knowledge of the Lord.

Many years ago I was invited to join Mensa, the worldwide organization for intellectuals with genius-level IQs. I declined because, for me, it would definitely have been a work of the flesh. Part of me was interested, but I had a greater desire to stay close to Jesus and the things of the Spirit. I was determined to be like a child and simply trust the Word of God. For me, even being a doorkeeper in the house of the Lord was preferable to achieving great success in the world apart from Him.

We are engaged in a great spiritual battle that we cannot ignore. The Word of God can tell us everything we need to know about the battle, the foes we face, the weapons at our disposal, and strategies for victory. That is why we need to discipline ourselves to stay in God's Word. All soldiers must go through discipline and training, and we are no different.

Ephesians 2:13 says that although we were once far away from God, the blood of Christ has brought us near. When we came near to the Lord, we experienced healing, salvation, and deliverance. He redeemed us from the hand of the devil. Now more than ever, our world needs this same redemption. Apart from the blood and name of Jesus, life is hopeless, meaningless, and full of utter chaos. Just take a look around at all the empty people living aimless and unfulfilled lives. Consider the nations of people around the world caught in spiritual darkness and oppressed by the fear and confusion of false religious systems. The world needs the blood of Jesus.

Study the Battlefield

Although the world needs Jesus, it is mostly under the sway of satan and the principalities of darkness. The key to our victory is the blood of the Lamb and the word of our testimony. We conquer through the blood.

According to most historical accounts, just before the Roman emperor Constantine won his pivotal victory against his rival, Maxentius, at the Milvian Bridge on October 28, 312, he had a vision of a cross superimposed on the sun, and the words *In hoc signo vince* ("In this sign, conquer"). Taking the vision literally, Constantine ordered his troops to paint crosses on their shields, and then went forth to win the battle. Although nominally a Christian before this victory, Constantine's vision marked the time of his "conversion." He became the first Christian emperor of Rome and made Christianity the official religion of the empire.

Unlike Constantine, ours is not primarily a physical or earthly battle. It is a spiritual battle for the earth and for the souls of men. The source of our success is the same as Constantine's, however. We still must conquer in the sign of the cross, which represents the blood sacrifice of Jesus, the Lamb of God. The battle between Constantine and Maxentius could represent the conflict between the people of God and the forces of the enemy, with the outcome determining the course of civilization.

Evil and godlessness have infected our culture, the same forces that have held other cultures and societies around the world in spiritual bondage for centuries. This is an ongoing struggle, not just a one-time event. It is important for us to know how to use our weapons because we need them on a daily basis. We need to keep on pleading the blood. We need to keep on walking in the Spirit. We need to keep on living in the Word of God. We need to keep on binding the powers of darkness away from over our society and our culture. We need to keep on watching and praying.

Just as important, we must understand the nature of the conflict. Good generals study the battlefield to get the lay of the land before committing their troops to battle. Likewise, it is important for us to study the battlefield before we enter the conflict. Increasingly, satan is marshaling the forces and institutions of society against the Lord, His Word, and His people. We are at war with the devil, and our culture is the battlefield.

Some time ago I saw a television interview of a young woman who was fired from her job as a teacher's aide because she wore a small cross. The school administration insisted that she take it off. She could not understand why, because she wore the cross everywhere. We're not talking about a big or fancy cross that would draw a lot of attention, but a small and rather inconspicuous one. Yet, she was told to remove it. When she refused, she was fired.

This did not occur in a communist or Muslim nation somewhere; this happened in the good old U. S. of A. I think it is likely that no one was truly offended by this woman's cross. The gurus of political correctness were *afraid* that someone *might* get offended. The only ones who were offended were satan and his demons because even that one little cross reminds them of what Jesus Christ did at Calvary. Forces of evil are at work trying to silence the voice and eliminate the influence of God's people in this country.

In recent years the Boy Scouts of America have come under fire because of their stance against homosexuality and against the approving of homosexual scoutmasters. For years the Boy Scout organization has been one of the participating programs receiving annual funds through the United Way. The Scouts use the money to conduct programs such as camps and swim parties for inner-city kids during the summer. Not long ago, the United Way in Miami/Dade County, Florida, informed the Boy Scouts a month before the annual drive was to begin that they would no longer be receiving any United Way funds. The reason: the Boy Scouts refused to set up training programs for the acceptance of homosexuality and diversity and for the teaching of gay views.

These are just two examples that reveal a little of the nature of the tremendous spiritual war that is raging in our society today. Traditional biblical and Christian values of morality are being savagely and systematically attacked by a spirit of hate, racism, anti-Semitism, and anti-Christian bigotry. The war is not going to go away. We are right in the middle of it, so we had better get our battle gear on and prepare to fight.

Gear Up for Battle

The Lord has given us a strategy for conquering the power of the enemy who would attack our children, our home, and our marriage. God wants us to be wise and alert to the tactics of the enemy, "lest satan should take advantage of us; for we are not ignorant of his devices" (2 Corinthians 2:11). He has also equipped us for the battle. In Ephesians 6:11, Paul tells us to "Put on the whole armor of God, that you may be able to stand against the wiles of the devil."

Having the proper weapons and equipment is vital for the success of any army in the field. The Persian Gulf War in 1991 and the more recent war in Iraq showed us all that America's military personnel are the most well-trained and best-equipped in the world. Soldiers on the ground in Iraq had everything from helmets, Kevlar bullet-proof vests, and semi-automatic rifles with computerized targeting systems to night-vision goggles and handheld GPS devices to locate their position with pinpoint accuracy.

Like the American soldiers in Iraq, we too have different kinds of armor and equipment as soldiers in God's army. Our first step in preparing for battle is to put on the armor that the Lord has given us. We have to take this seriously because we are in a war zone, and war is serious business. Being a soldier is not a lark.

In the movie *Private Benjamin*, Goldie Hawn portrays a rich and spoiled young Jewish woman who tries to escape her problems by joining the army. After seeing recruiting posters depicting pictures of foreign countries, she thought she would get to do a lot of fun travel and visit all sorts of resorts and such places. She expected the army to be a lark. What she found, however, was weeks of intensive basic training, strict discipline, and instruction in the techniques of modern war-fare. All the while she was protesting, "I didn't sign up for this!" Being a soldier turned out to be quite different from what she expected.

God does not want us to be like Private Benjamin; He wants us to know exactly what we "signed up" for as His soldiers. Under His command, we are to take on and conquer the powers of darkness. As we go forth to do battle for God's agenda and purposes, we will experience victory in our personal lives as well. Much of our success depends on being properly equipped for battle. That is why we need to put on our armor daily.

Paul describes our armor in detail:

1. *"Stand therefore, having girded your waist with truth"* (Ephesians 6:14a). Knowledge of the truth comes through the Word of God. Truth will counter the lies of the enemy.

2. *"...having put on the breastplate of righteousness"* (Ephesians 6:14b). Just as a breastplate guards our physical heart, righteousness guards our spiritual heart, keeping us pure and holy.

3. *"...and having shod your feet with the preparation of the gospel of peace"* (Ephesians 6:15). We wear the shoes of the gospel, which is the inspiration and motivation for everything we do. Just as our feet take us places, we take the gospel wherever we go.

4. *"...above all, taking the shield of faith with which you will be able to quench all the fiery darts of the wicked one"* (Ephesians 6:16). "Faith comes by hearing, and hearing by the Word of God" (Romans 10:17). Knowing God's Word builds our faith, and faith shields us against the personal attacks and accusations of the enemy.

5.   *"And take the helmet of salvation"* (Ephesians 6:17a). A helmet protects our head and brain, which houses our mind, the seat of our reasoning. It is through our minds that satan often attacks, but it is also through our minds that we understand and believe God's truth.

6.   *"...and the sword of the Spirit, which is the word of God"* (Ephesians 6:17b). A sword is both an offensive and a defensive weapon. God's Word defends us against the lies and deceptions of satan, but it also assaults and brings down his strongholds.

7.   *"Praying always with all prayer and supplication in the Spirit, being watchful to this end with all perseverance and supplication for all the saints"* (Ephesians 6:18). Prayer is like a battlefield commander staying in touch with headquarters: receiving new orders, coordinating the troops in the field, and requesting reinforcements and air support. Prayer is essential because it pulls everything else together.

Don't Back Down

Our armor is spiritual in nature because we are fighting a spiritual war. In Ephesians 6:12 Paul says, "For we do not wrestle against flesh and blood, but against principalities, against powers, against the rulers of the darkness of this age, against spiritual hosts of wickedness in the heavenly places." When we do battle against evil spirits we follow the example of our Lord. The moment Jesus returned from His 40-day fast in the wilderness and initiated His public ministry, He began confronting demonic spirits. As He preached and taught in the synagogues and in private homes and on the hillsides, demons often manifested, screaming out, "You are the Son of God!"

Jesus cast out demons, but He also ordered them to be silent about who He was.

The spiritual forces of darkness rise up to oppose the Lord and all who follow Him. They are quite adept at using societal influences to put pressure on God's people. Often, we are tempted to cut and run when our stand for Christ meets with resistance. When we stand up for traditional family values and against homosexuality, society labels us "intolerant bigots" and "hate-mongers." When we stand for sanctity of life and against abortion, society says we are trying to repress women and encouraging violence against abortion providers.

In the months following the war in Iraq, Lieutenant General William Boykin, head of the Pentagon's counterterrorism intelligence team and a committed Christian believer, was raked over the coals in the media because, while speaking to Christian congregations, he dared to characterize Islam as a false religion and the war on terrorism as a spiritual conflict. That these things are true was apparently beside the point. In exercising his constitutional rights of freedom of speech and freedom of religion, General Boykin offended the sensibilities of the politically correct elite and left many in the liberal establishment screaming for his head.

No matter how daunting or intimidating the opposition appears to be, as soldiers we are called to stand firm and never back down. That is what Jesus did. Jesus never caved in to the opposition. He never backpedaled or reversed Himself because someone did not like what He said. No one ever heard Jesus say, "Oh, Me! I'm sorry! I apologize for offending you! I realize now that it was not politically correct for Me to criticize other people's lifestyle choices. Go ahead, do what you want. Everything's okay. Adultery? Fine. Sodomy? No problem. Spiritual warfare? Nothing but superstition. I'm sorry I rocked the boat. I'll be more careful next time. It won't happen again."

That's not the Jesus *I* know! The Jesus I know stood firm and unshakable against all evil and wickedness until opposition grew to a tidal wave of hatred and hostility that slammed against Him with full force and nailed Him to a cross, only to fall in defeat after all when He rose from the dead. Jesus said, "As the Father has sent Me, I also send you" (John 20:21b). The Lord is training us to stand as He stood and fight as He fought. He is preparing us for warfare so that we can be watchmen to help bless and protect our homes, our marriages, our children, our neighborhoods, our cultures, and our nations. As soldiers of the Lord, we have to take responsibility for the territory assigned to us. Part of that responsibility is to understand the enemy we face.

Know Your Enemy

L et's take an inventory of some of the evil spirits that we may confront in battle.

And that very hour He cured many of infirmities, afflictions, and evil spirits; and to many blind He gave sight (Luke 7:21).

In the Greek, "evil spirits" in this verse is πονηρος πνευμά (*poneros pneuma*). The word *poneros* is derived from a word that means "anguish" or "pain," and another word that means "worthless," "corrupt," or "degenerate." In addition to "evil," *poneros* could be translated as "bad," "lewd," "malicious," or "wicked." This is the kind of malignant spirit that causes people to feel a burdensome yoke, as though a tremendous physical weight or toil is pressing on them. Once satan gets a foothold, he will take more and more until a person feels worn down by life. Sometimes people feel tired and worn down and doctors cannot find any physiological or psychological reason for it. The problem may be oppression by a *poneros* spirit.

> *When an unclean spirit goes out of a man, he goes through dry places, seeking rest, and finds none* (Matthew 12:43).

The Greek word for "unclean" here is ακαθαρτος (*akathartos*), which also means "impure," "lewd," and "foul." Its literal meaning is "not cleansed." This is a foul, filthy, vile spirit of the kind who drives people to do some unspeakable things. I read a while ago how the city of Toronto was devastated by the kidnapping and murder of a young girl around 12 years old. Her horribly abused and mutilated body was found a day and a half later, and authorities believe she was sexually assaulted and raped before she was killed. People ask, "How could anyone do such a thing?" Although there is enough evil in the human spirit alone to explain such wickedness, often an *akathartos* spirit may also be at work.

> *And behold, there was a woman who had a spirit of infirmity eighteen years, and was bent over and could in no way raise herself up. But when Jesus saw her, He called her to Him and said to her, "Woman, you are loosed from your infirmity." And He laid His hands on her, and immediately she was made straight, and glorified God* (Luke 13:11-13).

"Infirmity" here is ασθενεια (*astheneia*). The word also carries the meanings "feebleness," "sickness," and "weakness." This spirit manifests itself in weakness where a person lacks physical strength. Sometimes other disease symptoms are evident. Although disguised as an illness, this is an evil spirit. As these verses show, Jesus came to deliver us from our infirmities.

> *Now it happened, as we went to prayer, that a certain slave girl possessed with a spirit of divination met us, who brought her masters much profit by fortune-telling. This girl followed Paul and us, and cried out, saying, "These men are the servants of the Most High God, who proclaim to us the way of salvation." And this she did for many days. But Paul, greatly annoyed, turned and said to the spirit, "I command you in the name of Jesus Christ to come out of her." And he came out that very hour* (Acts 16:16-18).

In this instance, Paul encountered and cast out a spirit of divination. The word "divination" translates the Greek word Πυθωνος (*Puthonos*) or "Python," a proper name derived from "Putho," the region where the famed oracle of Delphi was located. Under the influence of this spirit, the slave girl served as a soothsayer and brought her masters much profit. People with a spirit of divination may say some things that are true and demonstrate knowledge that they could not otherwise know. The Holy Spirit will give us discernment regarding whether such a spirit is present. One way to tell the difference is that genuine prophecy, because it comes from the Holy Spirit, will always glorify Jesus; a spirit of divination will not.

> *So the great dragon was cast out, that serpent of old, called the devil and satan, who deceives the whole world; he was cast to the earth, and his angels were cast out with him* (Revelation 12:9).

This verse calls the devil a *deceiving* spirit. In Greek the word is πλαναω (*planao*), which means "to lead astray" or "to cause to wander." Through trickery and deceit, this spirit seeks to cause people to roam from safety, truth, or virtue. The danger to believers is that this spirit tries to seduce and entice them to turn away from the Word of God, from walking in obedience to the covenants of God, and from faithful involvement in the Body of Christ.

Many times, a deceiving spirit is behind a person's decision to join a cult. Sometimes it seduces men or women away from their spouses and into adulterous affairs by deceiving them into believing that the affair will meet a need in their life. The words or thoughts of a lying spirit may sound reasonable and logical, but they will not glorify Christ or agree with God's Word. This is one more reason why we need to get into and stay in the Scriptures. Thorough knowledge of the truth of God's Word will help us recognize the lies of a deceiving spirit.

Before serial killer Ted Bundy was executed in Florida, he gave an exclusive interview to Dr. James Dobson of Focus on the Family. In the interview, Bundy acknowledged that he had been ensnared by pornography at an early age, and his addiction to it was part of what drove him to murder young women. At some point, he was taken over by a demonic spirit. Here was a handsome, intelligent man with "guy-next-door" appeal who opened the door to the devil in his life and became one of the most monstrous murderers in our history.

Evil spirits will consume the unwary and destroy their lives. Simon Peter warned, "Be sober, be vigilant; because your adversary the devil walks about like a roaring lion, seeking whom he may devour" (1 Peter 5:8). We must always stay alert to the tactics of the enemy. The church is the vanguard of God's invasion force to free the world from the grip of satan's domination. He has given us the authority to overcome the devil and the responsibility to point people to Jesus so He can set them free. It is a responsibility we must take seriously.

Don't Shirk Your Responsibility

Satan was thoroughly and permanently defeated 2,000 years ago at the cross when Jesus bought our redemption with His blood. The devil's final destruction awaits the time of the last judgment, when he will be thrown into the "lake of fire" to be "tormented day and night forever and ever" (Revelation 20:10). For now, however, satan and his legions are living on borrowed time, and as their time grows short, they become more and more desperate. Although ultimately defeated, the powers of darkness are still a formidable force to reckon with.

As believers and soldiers in the army of the Lord, we have not only the authority but also the responsibility to bind the evil spirits and principalities and to use our spiritual armor and weapons to engage in warfare for the sake of our children and our fellow believers, as well as for all who do not yet know the Lord. Jesus commanded:

> *Go into all the world and preach the gospel to every creature. He who believes and is baptized will be saved; but he who does not believe will be condemned. And these signs will follow those who believe: In My name they will cast out demons; they will speak with new tongues; they will take up serpents; and if they drink anything deadly, it will by*

*no means hurt them; they will lay hands on the sick,
and they will recover* (Mark 16:15-18).

Our first priority is to preach the gospel of Jesus Christ
so that people who do not know Him can have the chance to
place their faith in Him and receive eternal life. Many individual believers and churches stop there. They know little
about spiritual gifts, signs and wonders, or spiritual warfare. I
have been to places where the need for spiritual warfare was
obvious to me, but when I asked some church leaders what
they were doing about it, they said, "Well, we don't really
believe in that stuff. We're more into praising and worshiping
the Lord."

I am all for praising and worshiping the Lord too, but
there also comes a time when we have to fight. The war is
already here. Since it is unavoidable, we have to decide how
we are going to deal with it. It is tempting sometimes to desert
the front lines and retreat to the rear. We cannot afford to shirk
our responsibility. Our children are being taken captive by
godless humanistic philosophies, evil music with violent,
obscene, anti-God, or anti-Christian lyrics, sexual perversions,
and social and moral values that are in direct opposition to
God's Word. Satanic spirits lie behind these influences. Someone in the church needs to learn to do warfare. We need to
learn to come together in agreement in Jesus' name and plead
His blood over our society.

Some people will never get delivered, but we can certainly so cleanse and protect our neighborhoods that when
sexual predators drive by looking for young children, as in
Toronto (and countless other places), they will not succeed
because holy angels of God are guarding the area with drawn
swords in response to the faithful and fervent prayers of

believing people. These kinds of things affect all of us. Our responsibility as believers is to take charge of the spiritual environment through intercession and pleading the blood. This is part of the anointing and the mantle that Jesus passed to His church.

It's great to enjoy the glory. It's wonderful to worship and praise the Lord, but there are also times when we have to get "down and dirty" and go to work. We have enjoyed a great meal and a tasty dessert, but now it is time to clean up. It may not be fun, but it needs to be done. We cannot simply keep sitting at the table. Cleanup is part of the celebration. Spiritual warfare comes with the Christian life. It is part of our training and part of our calling. Let's not shirk our responsibility. There is no room in God's army for slackers.

Power in the Blood

There is nothing the enemy fears more than the blood of Jesus. I believe satan fears the blood of Jesus more than he fears the Word of God. When the devil tempted Jesus in the wilderness, he even used Scripture in his efforts to turn the Lord to his will. Jesus is the living, incarnate Word of God, and satan attacked Him every chance he got, culminating in the crucifixion, where the devil thought he had finally won. Satan fears the blood of Jesus because he has no response to it; no answer and no counterfeit. He fears the blood of Jesus because it is the proof of his defeat and doom.

The blood sacrifice of the Lamb of God is the central theme of the Bible. The Bible contains 290 references to the love of God, over 400 references to the blood, and 1,300 references to the atonement—the saving work that Christ did on the cross. Every mention of sacrificial blood in the Old Testament, from the Passover blood on the Israelites' doorposts in Egypt to the blood sprinkled on the altar by the high priest on the Day of Atonement, points to the blood of Jesus on the cross in the New Testament. Jesus did a complete work at Calvary. Nothing remains to be done. His blood is sufficient to cleanse all the sins of mankind. One drop of His blood is enough to destroy satan's kingdom. That is why the devil fears the blood of Jesus. There is power in the blood.

The blood of Jesus has the power to draw us closer to God. We who were once far away from God have been brought near by the blood of Christ. His blood gives us the power to overcome every evil spirit and every weapon that is fashioned against us. It strengthens our faith and gives life to our prayers because it is only through the blood that we can come into the presence of the Father.

Blood is a living thing. Like our skin or stomach or heart, our blood is a living organ of our body. The life of every other organ depends on it. If we lose too much blood, we die. If blood circulation is cut off, those parts of the body that do not receive it will die. Our life is in our blood.

How much more, then, in the realm of the spirit does the blood of Jesus give us life! His blood avails for us, and we need to learn afresh to plead His blood over ourselves, over our families, and our children for health and protection, and for the power to overcome the forces of evil that war against us. There is power—and *victory*—in the blood of Jesus. The old gospel hymn states it so well:

> Would you be free from the burden of sin?
> There's power in the blood, power in the blood;
> Would you o'er evil a victory win?
> There's wonderful power in the blood.

Chapter Nine

Total Deliverance in the Lamb

I believe that today we are in a time of the greatest out-pouring of evil spirits in the history of the world. Demons that have been kept "on ice" so to speak for thousands of years are being released on the world in a flood. The devil is desperate because he knows his time is short.

One day years ago I had a vision in which I saw people running around frantically trying to escape from large vampire-like, bat-like creatures that were attacking them. The creatures had huge teeth like a shark's and were biting the people on their backs and necks. Then I saw letters on the backs of the bats. One bat was called divorce, another, addiction, and another, cancer. There were also other bats called abortion, suicide, and depression. All of them attacked relentlessly, biting and chewing on their victims who cried out in pain as they tried desperately to get away.

Demons thrive on negative energy. They love depression and discouragement. Nothing makes them happier than when husbands and wives argue. Negative energy makes them stronger.

In my vision, a woman stood up wearing a gorgeous white dress like a wedding gown. She was beautiful, but also looked somewhat fragile. As I watched, the woman raised her hands and started making flicking motions at the bats. Suddenly, the bats began to smoke, then burst into flames. Screaming and shrieking, they shriveled up and disappeared. With the bats gone, healing came to the people who had been under attack. The more I looked, the more I could see that a multitude of people—thousands upon thousands—had been totally delivered.

"Lord," I asked, "who is this woman?"

The Lord replied, "That is My bride. The world thinks My bride has no power. They have said all kinds of things against My church. She is My beloved. I am coming for My beloved, but before I do, every nation, as well as every demon, every principality, and even satan himself will know who My bride is."

Then I asked, "But Lord, what was she doing with her hands? What was the flicking motion all about? What did she do that made the bat-like creatures burn up and disappear?"

"Don't you understand?" the Lord answered. *"She was sprinkling My blood."*

The Truth Shall Make You Free

We live in a world where evil often appears invincible. Challenges, obstacles, and setbacks in life look insurmountable. Sometimes it seems as though the harder we try the worse our situation becomes. We begin to feel like Alice in Wonderland when she said, "The hurrier I go, the behinder I get!" Life can become a drag and a burden, with no visible way out. Such an attitude creates a ripe environment for demonic activity to flourish.

No matter how hopeless a situation may appear, we never know the truth about any situation until we hear from Jesus. Not only is He the source of truth, He *is* truth. Jesus told His disciples, "I am the way, the truth, and the life. No one comes to the Father except through Me" (John 14:6). Even a "hopeless" situation is never hopeless when we see it through Jesus' eyes.

Without truth there can be no freedom. That is why communism, fascism, Nazism, and other totalitarian systems through the centuries have hated the Bible. They fear truth because truth leads to freedom. Totalitarian states control their citizens through fear and ignorance. They become masters of misinformation in order to keep the people from knowing the truth. In the case of religious totalitarian states, such as those with radical, fundamentalist Islamic governments, the leaders themselves are caught up in the ignorance, zealously propagating a false religion they believe to be true.

Millions of people worldwide are in spiritual or even social and political bondage and need to be freed. Freedom comes in knowing the truth, and truth is found in the Word of God because the Word of God points to Jesus who is truth. Jesus tried to explain this to a group of Jews who were having trouble understanding:

Then Jesus said to those Jews who believed Him, "If you abide in My word, you are My disciples indeed. And you shall know the truth, and the truth shall make you free." They answered Him, "We are Abraham's descendants, and have never been in bondage to anyone. How can you say, 'You will be made free?' " Jesus answered them, "Most assuredly, I say to you, whoever commits sin is a slave of sin.

*And a slave does not abide in the house forever, but
a son abides forever. Therefore if the Son makes you
free, you shall be free indeed"* (John 8:31-36).

People without Christ are in sin, and sin is bondage,
darkness, and ignorance. Christ brings freedom, light, and
knowledge of the truth. The way we *stay* in the truth is by
abiding in His Word.

Part of our freedom in Christ is deliverance, whether
from pain or disease, addiction, demonic oppression or possession, emotional or psychological problems, mental illness,
anger, hate, bitterness, or whatever. Once people truly understand the freedom that is available in Jesus, they rush to get
delivered.

Once when I was holding a series of evangelistic and
healing meetings in the African nation of Zambia, we con-
ducted a deliverance service. These African people had gone
to witch doctors all their lives, even though Christian missionaries had evangelized their country beginning a century earlier. Many of these people knew Jesus, but knew nothing of His
power to deliver because no one had ever told them.

The missionaries had said, "You must believe in Jesus,
but don't pray for healing or for the casting out of demons.
Jesus does not do those things anymore. Satan and his demons
are really just figments of the imagination. Jesus was simply
trying to give us spiritual truth."

A century later, I was standing in front of thousands of
Zambians who needed deliverance of some kind or another.
With some of them, demons were practically hanging from
their fingertips. Witch doctors had spoken all kinds of curses,
partly to frighten people from coming to the meetings. Many

of those witch doctors were satan worshipers. They were so steeped in the occult that they actually possessed a certain amount of evil power, just like Jannes and Jambres, the magicians of Pharaoh who were able to duplicate some of Moses' miracles with their magic arts.

I stood before those people and said, "Don't you dare be afraid of those witch doctors. Don't you dare be afraid of satan." As I began casting out evil spirits, hundreds of people began to fall to the floor. Some were slain in the Spirit while others had been put on the floor by the evil spirits in them. Many of these who had given themselves over to evil, casting evil spells having to do with animals, suddenly started acting like those animals. Then the evil spirits shrieked and came out of them.

When the native pastors and leaders saw this, they said to me, "Brother Mahesh, we have never seen anything like this before! You take such authority over these evil spirits, but all the other preachers and missionaries who came before you told us that Jesus did not do this kind of thing anymore. When our people were sick and hurting, we did not know what to tell them, so they would go to the witch doctors and get the spells and witchcraft medicines to take. We are so glad you have shown us that Jesus is alive, that He is the Lord, and that we do not have to be afraid of these witch doctors any longer! *If only those missionaries who came 100 years ago had told us the things you are telling us, our whole nation would have turned to Jesus!*"

There is total deliverance in Jesus. He is the truth, and the truth makes us free.

Household Salvation

When Jesus died on the cross, He paid with His blood the price of our salvation, our deliverance, and our healing, both for ourselves as well as for our homes, our marriages, and our children. Although each person must individually place his or her faith in Christ to be saved, we as parents and family leaders can cover our homes and families under the protective cloak of the blood of Jesus to create an atmosphere conducive to faith that also restricts the enemy's freedom to work.

This principle of "household salvation" is illustrated in the preparations the Israelites made for the first Passover and their approaching departure from Egypt:

Now the Lord spoke to Moses and Aaron in the land of Egypt, saying, "This month shall be your beginning of months; it shall be the first month of the year to you. Speak to all the congregation of Israel, saying: 'On the tenth day of this month every man shall take for himself a lamb, according to the house of his father, a lamb for a household. And if the household is too small for the lamb, let him and his neighbor next to his house take it according to the number of the persons; according to each man's need you shall make your count for the lamb. Your lamb shall be without blemish, a male of the first year. You may take it from the sheep or from the goats.'

Now you shall keep it until the fourteenth day of the same month. Then the whole assembly of the congregation of Israel shall kill it at twilight. And they shall take some of the blood and put it on the two doorposts and on the lintel of the houses where they eat it." (Exodus 12:1-7).

When God told Moses and Aaron, "This month shall be your beginning of months," He meant, "This is where everything begins for you. Your life as a nation begins on this date, when the Passover lamb is given." This would be the most significant event in their history, the day the Israelites were transformed from slaves into the people of God.

On the tenth day of the month, the head of each home was to "take for himself a lamb...a lamb for a household." If one family was too small for a whole lamb by itself, it could share a lamb with the family next door. The point is that the blood of one lamb was sufficient for everyone in the household.

That is what I mean by "household salvation." If you are a child of God through faith in Jesus Christ, you have every right to claim your husband, your wife, your children, your grandchildren—anyone in your household—for covering under Jesus' blood. You can stand boldly before God and say, "Lord, I'm interceding for my children that none of them will be lost, but each one washed in the blood of Jesus." One lamb covers an entire household; not one of your loved ones will be missing.

This is something we need to claim by faith, even when all visible evidence seems to point to the contrary. Jesus Christ offers total deliverance, and we need to be faithful and claim everyone in our household for Him in His name. Our God is big enough to save our spouses, our children, our grandchildren, our aunts and uncles, our brothers and sisters, our nieces, nephews, and cousins—indeed, everyone in our families—and renew them in the Spirit of God.

It doesn't matter whether your children are physically under your roof or not. They can be thousands of miles away and you can still cover them. I have seen instant deliverances of people halfway around the world in response to the covering and intercession of faithful family members.

One mother and father I remember asked me to pray for their young adult daughter who had been in France for a couple of years. They had not spoken directly with her in months, but had learned through other sources that she had gotten involved in drugs and a generally unhealthy lifestyle. This was a young woman who had been raised as a Christian, but had gotten on the wrong track. Her parents and I prayed together. Later they told me joyfully that two hours after our prayer, they received a phone call from their daughter, who was in tears and said she was ready to come home. She did return home and was fully restored to her family and to the Lord.

Just as the blood of one lamb covered an Israelite household that first Passover night in Egypt, so the blood of the one and only Lamb of God can cover us and all our households today.

The lamb whose blood was to be spread on the lintels and doorposts had to be "without blemish;" in other words, spotless and perfect with no flaws. Likewise, Jesus, the Lamb of God, was spotless and without blemish. Even though He was born as a human, His blood was not contaminated by the sinful nature of mankind. As the Son of God, Jesus' blood was pure and sinless, and therefore powerful to cleanse our sin and bring us salvation.

From Slavery to Royalty

God also specified a specific manner in which the Israelites were to eat the Passover lamb:

Then they shall eat the flesh on that night; roasted in fire, with unleavened bread and with bitter herbs

*they shall eat it. Do not eat it raw, nor boiled at all
with water, but roasted in fire; its head with its legs
and its entrails. You shall let none of it remain until
morning, and what remains of it until morning you
shall burn with fire. And thus you shall eat it: with
a belt on your waist, your sandals on your feet, and
your staff in your hand. So you shall eat it in haste.
It is the Lord's Passover* (Exodus 12:8-11).

The lamb had to be thoroughly roasted so that there was
no juice or blood. God had forbidden them to eat blood
because the life is in the blood. They were to eat the roasted
lamb with unleavened bread and bitter herbs. Unleavened
bread, you remember, symbolized the absence of sin as well as
the haste of their departure from Egypt. They did not have
time to let the leaven rise before baking the bread, so they left
it out. Bitter herbs reminded them of the bitterness of their
days of slavery—days they were about to leave behind forever. As such, the bitter herbs also served as a reminder of their
testimony: "God delivered us; what a mighty God we have!"

A testimony is something we carry with us all the time.
It helps us remember where we came from. At first, we were
nothing, lost and bound in sin, but now we have been bought
with the blood of Jesus and brought near to God. Once we
were homeless outcasts, but now we are citizens of the kingdom of God and members of His royal family, a company of
kings and priests. Remembering where we came from also
helps us remember what Jesus did for us.

When the Israelites sat down to eat the Passover meal,
they were to be dressed for travel on a moment's notice. When
their deliverance came, it would come quickly. A belt around
the waist made it possible to tuck the hems of long robes out

of the way of their legs so they could walk unhindered. This is where the phrase "gird up your loins" comes from. Sandals, apart from being a symbol of freedom since slaves most often were barefoot, also were necessary for protecting their feet as they walked long distances. A staff in hand meant they were ready to step out the moment the word was given. It meant they were on their way to the promised land.

Total Deliverance

Looking at the Israelites' situation before they left Egypt, it would seem they had no hope in the natural. Egypt was the largest and most powerful empire on earth at that time. Her material wealth was almost beyond comprehension and her army was second to none. No other kingdom in the area dared to go up against Egypt. Israel standing up to the might of Egypt was like Bangladesh facing off with the United States. Their deliverance would have been beyond hopeless except that God was on their side.

God said, "You have been slaves for 400 years, but I am going to deliver you. Overnight you are going to be free."

Many of the Israelites probably wanted to ask, "How are You going to do it, Lord? How are You going to free us from four centuries of oppression? Our Egyptian masters have owned us, robbed us, and worked us to death. Some of us have been maimed in the quarry pits and on the construction sites. They can do whatever they wish to us. Where is Your army, Lord, that can defeat the army of Pharaoh? How will You deliver us?"

God said, "You are moving out tonight, *all* of you."

This was no small project. Counting women and children, the Israelites probably numbered 3 or 4 million. Try to imagine what it would take to move 4 million people. I live in Charlotte, North Carolina, a city of around 1 million. The exodus was the equivalent of completely evacuating four cities the size of Charlotte!

How would you carry out such a task? It's not just the able-bodied you would have to be concerned about. Out of the 4 million people in those cities, how many would be in the hospitals? How many would be on dialysis? How many would have heart conditions or respiratory illnesses? How many amputees would there be? How many blind people would there be? How many babies or elderly people would there be who could not walk without assistance?

First of all, you would need thousands of ambulances, thousands of doctors, and tens of thousands of nurses to take care of the kidney patients, the liver patients, the cancer patients, and so on. You would need 10,000 tractor trailers to carry the food for four 4 million people, and another 10,000 to cart the water.

Out of 4 million people living in slavery under harsh conditions, the Israelites certainly must have had many aged, maimed, infirm, and sick people, not to mention little children who could not take care of themselves. Were these to be left behind?

God said, "*All* of you are leaving."

The lamb's blood smeared on the doorposts not only preserved the Israelites from death; it brought them *total* deliverance. Psalm 105:37 says that when the Lord led the children of Israel out of Egypt, there were "none feeble" among them. In other words, God healed all their infirmities before they left! Blindness, deafness, asthma, cancer, heart disease, missing limbs, crippled feet—all were cured overnight! When the

Israelites walked out of Egypt that night, they walked out healed, whole, rich, and free—*totally delivered*!

For the Israelites, the lamb's blood was a symbol. Today, we have the real thing: the precious, priceless blood of Jesus that can still bring total deliverance. He is the Lamb of God who takes away the sin of the world. His blood changes and transforms us, flowing as a life-giving river to renew and refresh us after years of spiritual bondage and the yokes of oppression and depression. It is time to exercise our faith and let the power of His blood be loosed in us, in our families, and in our churches. We are the bride of Christ, and through us the healing and delivering blood of Jesus should flow to all the nations. Let's gird up our loins, put on our sandals and grab our staff, because we're headed for the promised land!

Joy, Glory, and Holiness

Total deliverance in the Lamb brings us into entirely new dimensions of understanding and intimacy with the Father. Three specific benefits that arise are a greater abundance of joy, a higher experience of glory, and a deeper growth in holiness. Simon Peter addresses these three benefits in his first letter:

> *That the genuineness of your faith, being much more precious than gold that perishes, though it is tested by fire, may be found to praise, honor, and glory at the revelation of Jesus Christ, whom having not seen you love. Though now you do not see Him, yet believing, you rejoice with joy inexpressible and full of glory"* (1 Peter 1:7-8).

Inexpressible joy is joy that bubbles over, an overflowing joy that cannot be described. Such joy is "full of glory." Glory is found in the presence of the Lord, so the closer we get to God, the closer we get to the glory, and the closer we get to the glory, the more our joy increases. There is joy in the presence of the Lord. People caught up in "religion" rarely know true joy. There is no presence of God in empty religion. Without God's presence there is no glory, and without glory there is no joy.

> *Receiving the end of your faith—the salvation of your souls. Of this salvation the prophets have inquired and searched carefully, who prophesied of the grace that would come to you, searching what, or what manner of time, the Spirit of Christ who was in them was indicating when He testified before-hand the sufferings of Christ and the glories that would follow* (1 Peter 1:9-11).

Another source of our joy is the knowledge and assurance that we have received "the salvation of our souls." Jesus accomplished this for us through His sufferings: the mocking, the beating, the crown of thorns, and the cross. He endured these things for the glories that He knew would follow, not only for Him, but also for us as well. The Lord wants us to enter the glory, and He has gone before us to open the way.

> *To them it was revealed that, not to themselves, but to us they were ministering the things which now have been reported to you through those who have preached the gospel to you by the Holy Spirit sent from heaven—things which angels desire to look into* (1 Peter 1:12).

There are some things that are so awesome and so full of glory that even the angels do not comprehend. One of these is the mystery of salvation. Since the angels have never been lost, they have no concept of what it means to be saved. All the prophets from Moses to Malachi received tantalizing hints of the glory that was to come through Jesus Christ. They did not understand it much better than the angels, but they knew something awesome was about to happen that would release the glory of God on earth. We have the advantage over them in that we have received the full revelation—Jesus Christ in all His glory—which came to us by the preaching of the gospel in the power of the Holy Spirit.

> *Therefore gird up the loins of your mind, be sober, and rest your hope fully upon the grace that is to be brought to you at the revelation of Jesus Christ; as obedient children, not conforming yourselves to the former lusts, as in your ignorance; but as He who called you is holy, you also be holy in all your conduct, because it is written, "Be holy, for I am holy"* (1 Peter 1:13-16).

Peter says to "gird up the loins of your mind." In other words, "Get your act together!" We need to rest our hope *fully* on God's grace as revealed to us by Jesus. There is no other hope we can rest on; it is the grace of God or nothing. The Lord has called us to a life of holiness, which means being obedient to His will and His Word, and turning away from the "former lusts"—the things of the flesh and the devil—that characterized our lives before we knew Christ.

Holiness is not an exercise of religion; it is an exercise of the anointing. Some people hear the word "holy" and they think, "Oh, that means women cannot wear pants or makeup, and men have to keep their hair short." No, that's not holiness. Holiness is a grace gift of the Spirit that enables us to say "no" to unrighteousness, "no" to evil speaking, "no" to lust, "no" to the flesh, and "yes" to all the things that please God and characterize His children. Holiness is the process of being sanctified, in which we are set apart—made holy—for God's purposes.

Nothing But the Blood

In the end, God's great purpose for us is that we be pure and holy, a fit and proper bride for His Son.

> *And if you call on the Father, who without partiality judges according to each one's work, conduct yourselves throughout the time of your stay here in fear; knowing that you were not redeemed with corruptible things, like silver or gold, from your aimless conduct received by tradition from your fathers, but with the precious blood of Christ, as of a lamb without blemish and without spot* (1 Peter 1:17-19).

We have been redeemed by nothing less than the precious blood of Jesus. Nothing less would have been sufficient. He is the Lamb of God without spot or blemish, slain before the foundation of the world. That which the Israelites partook of symbolically, we partake of in reality. Jesus shed His precious blood for you us so that we can rest today secure in the grace of God.

We cannot rest on our works or on our goodness. Only one thing can redeem our souls from sin; only one thing can silence the devil's accusations and turn away his attacks: the blood of Jesus. Nothing else will do. This old gospel hymn sums it up well:

What can wash away my sin? Nothing but the
blood of Jesus;
What can make me whole again? Nothing but the
blood of Jesus.

For my pardon this I see, Nothing but the blood
of Jesus;
For my cleansing, this my plea, Nothing but the
blood of Jesus.
Nothing can for sin atone, Nothing but the blood
of Jesus;
Naught of good that I have done, Nothing but the
blood of Jesus.
This is all my hope and peace, Nothing but the
blood of Jesus;
This is all my righteousness, Nothing but the blood
of Jesus.
Oh! Precious is the flow, That makes me white
as snow;
No other fount I know, Nothing but the blood
of Jesus.

The precious blood of Jesus, poured out on Calvary is what we are resting on today. Through the eternal ages in heaven we will see a Lamb as freshly slain standing at the right hand of the Father, slain before the foundation of the world, yet always freshly slain. That Lamb is Jesus Christ of Nazareth.

The Power of the Blood Covering

There is life, power, protection, and total deliverance in the blood of the Lamb. His blood is sufficient to save our souls and heal every disease or infirmity. When His blood covers us, we are completely safe.

1. There is *protection* under the covering of the blood. "Now the blood shall be a sign for you on the houses where you are. And when I see the blood, I will pass over

you; and the plague shall not be on you to destroy you when I strike the land of Egypt" (Exodus 12:13).

2.   There is *salvation* under the covering of the blood. "And He said to them, 'This is My blood of the new covenant, which is shed for many' " (Mark 14:24). "Nor is there salvation in any other, for there is no other name under heaven given among men by which we must be saved" (Acts 4:12).

3.   There is *healing* under the covering of the blood. "But He was wounded for our transgressions, He was bruised for our iniquities; the chastisement for our peace was upon Him, and by His stripes we are healed" (Isaiah 53:5).

4.   There is *provision* under the covering of the blood. "He also brought them out with silver and gold" (Psalm 105:37a).

5.   There is *life* under the covering of the blood. "And there was none feeble among His tribes" (Psalm 105:37b). "I have come that they may have life, and that they may have it more abundantly" (John 10:10b).

6.   There is *forgiveness* under the covering of the blood. "And according to the law almost all things are purified with blood, and without shedding of blood there is no remission" (Hebrews 9:22).

7.   There is *cleansing* under the covering of the blood. "But if we walk in the light as He is in the light, we have fellowship with one another, and the blood of Jesus Christ His Son cleanses us from all sin" (1 John 1:7).

8.   There is *redemption* under the covering of the blood. "In Him we have redemption through His blood, the forgiveness

of sins, according to the riches of His grace" (Ephesians 1:7).

9. There is *justification* under the covering of the blood. "Much more then, having now been justified by His blood, we shall be saved from wrath through Him" (Romans 5:9).

10. There is *sanctification* under the covering of the blood. "Therefore Jesus also, that He might sanctify the people with His own blood, suffered outside the gate" (Hebrews 13:12).

11. There is *peace* under the covering of the blood. "For it pleased the Father that in Him all the fullness should dwell, and by Him to reconcile all things to Himself, by Him, whether things on earth or things in heaven, having made peace through the blood of His cross" (Colossians 1:19-20).

12. There is *washing* in the blood. "And from Jesus Christ, the faithful witness, the firstborn from the dead, and the ruler over the kings of the earth. To Him who loved us and washed us from our sins in His own blood" (Revelation 1:5).

13. There is *overcoming* power in the blood. "And they overcame him by the blood of the Lamb and by the word of their testimony, and they did not love their lives to the death" (Revelation 12:11).

14. There is *speaking* power in the blood, crying out for mercy, grace and blessing on our behalf. "To Jesus the Mediator of the new covenant, and to the blood of sprinkling that speaks better things than that of Abel" (Hebrews 12:24).

15. There is *accessing* ability in the blood, allowing us into the presence of God. "Therefore, brethren, having boldness to enter the Holiest by the blood of Jesus" (Hebrews 10:19).

Chapter Ten

VICTORY THROUGH
THE PASSOVER LAMB

When Jesus of Nazareth appeared on the scene, walking the hills of Galilee, preaching, teaching, and healing in the towns and villages along the Sea of Galilee and in Judea, He was the fulfillment of centuries of prophetic anticipation. Every prophetic book in the Old Testament contains prophetic references to Jesus, either symbolically or directly.

Even though he appears in the New Testament, John the Baptist was the last in this Old Testament prophetic tradition. John's powerful preaching and unusual lifestyle drew a lot of attention because the Jews had not seen or heard a true prophet in 400 years. Even the Jewish religious leaders in Jerusalem were curious enough about John to send priests and Levites to find out who he was. John quoted Isaiah when he said, "I am the voice of one crying in the wilderness: make straight the way of the Lord" (John 1:23). By his own testimony, John was a messenger, a forerunner to announce the coming of the Messiah.

John answered them, saying, "I baptize with water,
but there stands One among you whom you do not

*know. It is He who, coming after me, is preferred
before me, whose sandal strap I am not worthy to
loose." These things were done in Bethabara beyond
the Jordan, where John was baptizing. The next day
John saw Jesus coming toward him, and said,
"Behold! The Lamb of God who takes away the sin
of the world!"* (John 1:26-29).

"Behold the Lamb of God who takes away the sin of the
world." How we need to let the truth of that statement penetrate deep into our spirit! Jesus Christ is our Passover Lamb,
and by His sacrifice—by the pouring out of His blood—the
sins of the world are taken away. That means there is no one
on earth who cannot receive the blessing of having their sins
forgiven through faith in the Lord Jesus Christ. There is no
family on earth that Jesus did not come to bless and release
from every oppression and to set every captive free. He is the
Lamb of God!

Hold the Word Dear

I will never forget the time when Bonnie and I flew into an
area of Zaire called Kikwit, which was one of the major
locations of the Ebola virus outbreakout. It was deep in the
interior of the country, part of the region author Joseph Con-
rad called "the heart of darkness." The Mission Aviation Fellowship flew us there over hundreds of miles of African
terrain. As we looked down, we saw thousands of people, like
ants, walking toward the same place we were going.

After we landed, I asked one of the local pastors, "What
is happening here? Where are all these people going? Is there
some big football game or government event taking place?"

He replied, "They are all coming to your meeting."

People came who had walked for seven days through the African bush, three of those days without food, just so they could hear the word of the Lord. How many of us would walk for days and hundreds of miles, enduring hunger and thirst and burning heat, just to get one little word of strength, comfort, and release?

It is impossible for us to overestimate the importance of holding dear the Word of God. People's eternal welfare may depend on how we handle the Bible and the gospel message. That first night in Kikwit, my message was very simple: I held up Jesus Christ to them. The theme of my message was, "Behold the Lamb of God, who takes away the sins of the whole world."

On that first night, over 50,000 people attended, and the numbers grew from there. In the middle of my preaching, a young boy began walking up the center aisle. By the time he got half way, the whole crowd was murmuring, and then they began to cheer. Puzzled, I asked one of the local leaders, "Why are they doing that?" It turned out that this boy, about nine years old, had been crippled from birth. The whole town knew about him because he was well known as a beggar for alms. Now this great crowd, who had known this boy all his life and knew that in all that time he had never walked, saw him walking as if he had been doing it for years!

This young boy was able to behold the Lamb of God. He connected with the One who is the same yesterday, today, and forever. When he came under the power of the blood of the Lamb, he was healed instantly and began walking for the first time in his life. By faith, that young boy connected with the Lamb of God and received his healing.

People in this remote region had never seen television. They barely even had electricity. That did not matter. God's healing and saving power are just as real and just as potent in the deepest and darkest parts of the Zaire Congo as in the modern, brightly-lit, and high-tech cities of the United States.

Each of us as believers has a calling from the Lord to exercise our faith for the covering of our families, our loved ones, our neighbors, and the world. We need to intercede for revival to come to America. We need to intercede for revival to come to Russia. We need to intercede for the people of Saudi Arabia and Indonesia and Iraq and Iran and Afghanistan to be saved. We need to intercede for India and Pakistan and Egypt and Israel and Palestine to come to know the Lord. Wherever we are, we can exercise our faith. May the nations behold the Lamb of God and believe. Jesus is the Passover Lamb. How desperately we need in this hour to receive His Word afresh and hold it dear. God's Word is eternal, yet ever new and fresh. It never goes out of style or becomes passé. He always has a new word for us if we will only listen.

We Know the End of the Story

We are engaged in a great spiritual battle between good and evil, between the principalities and powers of darkness and the Lord of the ages. The enemy marshals human resources to carry out his schemes against God and His people. No matter how fiercely the conflict rages, we already know the end of the story: as children of the Lord, we are on the winning side. Nevertheless, our foe is formidable, and he would like nothing better than to make us believe that our fight is hopeless. One of his most popular tactics is to try to discourage us to the point of quitting by using intimidation, fear, or shock.

Few scenes I have witnessed in recent years have moved me as much as watching film footage from Ground Zero as bodies were exhumed from the debris of the World Trade Center. Months after the attack, rescuers were still pulling out the bodies of the brave police officers and firefighters, both men and women, who gave their lives helping others escape the burning towers.

Evil touched America on September 11, 2001 in a way as never before. Demonic evil took tangible shape in the form of fanatic extremists who hijacked passenger airliners and crashed them into those towers, as well as into the Pentagon in Washington, D.C., in the maniacal desire to wantonly kill thousands of Americans. In reality, those terrorists and the ones who sponsored them declared war on the world, because citizens of many nations, not just America, were victims of that attack.

I was particularly touched by the film documentary made by two French brothers who happened to be on the scene that day and filmed what went on inside the World Trade Center. There were firefighters waiting on the ground floor of one of the towers, ready to go up. While people who worked in the tower rushed downstairs in a flood trying to escape, these resolute professionals were on their way up to help those who could not get down. Providing a horrifying backdrop to these scenes in the documentary were the sounds of human bodies impacting the ground as people trapped on the upper stories jumped to escape the flames.

The faces of those firefighters—men and women—were set and determined. They were going up when everyone else was running down. You could tell by their faces that most of them knew they were going to die, but they were going up anyway. They were true heroes.

Their resolve in the face of certain death reminded me of Jesus, who resolutely set His face like flint to go to Jerusalem and die. He was the greatest hero of all who, as our Passover Lamb, willingly went into the jaws of death and hell for you and me. "Greater love has no one than this," Jesus said, "than to lay down one's life for his friends" (John 15:13). Jesus Christ is our greatest friend. He rode into Jerusalem on a donkey, gave Himself up to the horror of the cross, and endured the even deeper horror of becoming sin on our behalf. When He died, sin's power and hold on us died with Him. Three days later, He rose from the dead in triumph. At the end of the day, He won the victory. Because Jesus gave Himself totally to death for us, we can experience total victory through Him, our Passover Lamb.

Seeing Jesus in the Passover

Every Palm Sunday we celebrate Jesus' triumphal entry into Jerusalem. Hailed by the crowd, He would die on the cross less than a week later, at Passover. By God's plan, Jesus was the final and ultimate Passover Lamb.

The message of the gospel and the progression of God's redemptive plan are revealed symbolically in the feasts of Israel. Passover is the first of the three feast seasons in the Jewish calendar. As a memorial to the Jews of their deliverance from slavery in Egypt, Passover is always celebrated on the 14th day of the month of *Nisan*, which corresponds to March-April on the Julian calendar. This is the time of the barley harvest. The most important of all the Jewish festivals,

Passover represents God's first encounter with His covenant people.

The Passover festival season has three parts: Passover, Unleavened Bread, and Firstfruits. Jesus celebrated Passover, and then went to Calvary, where He was crucified. His death is symbolized in the Feast of Unleavened Bread. Firstfruits symbolizes His resurrection, with the promise of future resurrection for all who believe in Him. "But now Christ is risen from the dead, and has become the firstfruits of those who have fallen asleep" (1 Corinthians 15:20).

Fifty days after Firstfruits is Pentecost, during the wheat harvest in the month of *Sivan* (May-June), which commemorates the giving of the Law on Mount Sinai. The Holy Spirit descended on Pentecost, and a great harvest of souls ensued.

After Pentecost, in the month of *Tishri* (September-October), is the Feast of Tabernacles. This feast is divided into Trumpets, the Day of Atonement, and Tabernacles. These symbolize, respectively, the defeat of the enemy, the purifying of the bride of Christ, and the second coming of *Yeshua Ha Maschia*, the King of Glory.

During the Passover season, the head of each household chose the lamb for the Passover on the 10th day of the month. At twilight on the 14th day of the month, the lamb was slaughtered. This allowed five days to ensure that the lamb chosen was without blemish. On Palm Sunday, Jesus came into Jerusalem, was "examined" by the priests and other leaders, and found to have no fault or blemish. On the fifth day after, He was nailed to a cross and slain. That which the yearly Passover lamb foreshadowed in symbol, Jesus fulfilled in reality.

Understanding the ritual of Passover helps us understand major truths regarding what Jesus did for us and for all the world when He died on the cross. When the Passover lamb was slaughtered, its blood was caught in a basin at the foot of the doorstep. Then, with a branch of hyssop, the blood was brushed on both sides of the doorpost and on the lintel above. This was done at twilight on the 14th day of *Nisan*. The Hebrew day was measured from sunset to sunset, which means that at this time of the year, their day began around 6:00 p.m. They would kill the lamb at 3:00, cook it, and then spread the blood on the doorposts and lintel. At 6:00 the family would enter the house through the bloodstained door, where they would be protected from the plague of death. There they would share together the meal that symbolized their deliverance.

There were precise instructions for preparing the lamb. First of all, it had to be roasted thoroughly. Second, it had to be completely consumed. Nothing could be left over for the next day. Third, not one bone of the lamb was to be broken. Finally, the lamb was to be placed on a wooden spit shaped like a cross so that its body could be spread open.

On that first Passover night, as the Israelites ate their meal, the death angel swept through the land of Egypt. As he passed from door to door, he sought to enter every household. If the entrance was covered by blood, the angel of death could not enter, but had to pass over that house. That is why this feast is called the Passover. The angel of death passed over the houses that were covered by the blood of the lamb. The blood was a seal that protected the people inside. Judgment came on any house not covered by the blood, and the firstborn of that household died.

This was the Lord's Passover. The Lord used the blood of the lamb to save His people from death. That blood made atonement for the sins of that household. Everyone was covered—not just the father and mother, but the children and any others who were part of the household.

In a like manner, Jesus, the Lamb of God, was stretched open on cross-shaped wood. In death He was consumed completely, but none of His bones were broken. His blood made atonement for all who enter His "house" through faith. All who are thus covered by His blood are protected from the judgment of death.

Over the years, the annual Passover celebration became a time of great joy, praise, and adoration in the worship of God. For the Jews it represented deliverance from oppression. Every curse was broken: the curse of slavery, the curse of poverty, and the curse of disease and affliction. During the time of the Temple, the Levites would lead the people in singing the psalms of David, particularly Psalms 113 through 118. The Levites would sing one line of the psalm, and the people would sing the next line. Often, their singing was accompanied by musical instruments such as trumpets, harps, flutes, tambourines, and cymbals.

Psalm 118:24 says, "This is the day the Lord has made; we will rejoice and be glad in it." This is talking about Passover. For us, the blood of Jesus applies every day, so every day we can say, "This is the day the Lord has made; we will rejoice and be glad in it."

Although the lambs slain on Passover symbolized the covering of sin, lamb's blood had no power to actually take sin away. God sent prophets to His people to reveal to them that a future day was coming when the Lord Himself would provide an offering, a perfect human Lamb without spot or blemish, who would deal once and for all with the problems of sin and death.

Man of Sorrows

No Old Testament prophet speaks more eloquently about the Lamb of God than does Isaiah. The 53rd chapter of Isaiah is one of the most beautiful and moving passages in all of Scripture. It is classic. Years ago I laid hold of this chapter as my ministry with the mentally handicapped began. Read it carefully, meditate on it prayerfully, and it will help you connect with the Lion of the tribe of Judah, the Lamb of God who died but rose again.

Who has believed our report? And to whom has the arm of the Lord been revealed? For He shall grow up before Him as a tender plant, and as a root out of dry ground. He has no form or comeliness; and when we see Him, there is no beauty that we should desire Him. He is despised and rejected by men, a Man of sorrows and acquainted with grief. And we hid, as it were, our faces from Him; He was despised, and we did not esteem Him. Surely He has borne our griefs and carried our sorrows; yet we esteemed Him stricken, smitten by God, and afflicted. But He was wounded for our transgressions, He was bruised for our iniquities; the chastisement for our peace was upon Him, and by His stripes we are healed. All we like sheep have gone astray; we have turned, every one, to his own way; And the Lord has laid on Him the iniquity of us all. He was oppressed and He was afflicted, yet He opened not His mouth; He was led as a lamb to the slaughter, and as a sheep before its shearers is silent, so He opened not His mouth. He was taken from prison and from judgment, and who will declare His generation? For He was cut off from the land of the living; for the transgressions of My people He was stricken (Isaiah 53:1-8).

Jesus was wounded for our transgressions and bruised for our iniquities. It is by His stripes that we are healed physically, mentally, emotionally, and spiritually. His healing is for us as well as for our children. It depends on faith, not feelings. We could be really upbeat today and down in the dumps tomorrow. That does not matter. Our healing is based on the living Word of God. Heaven and earth may pass away, but God's Word will stand forever, and we can stand on that.

Breaking the Curse

Healing the sick and casting out demons were regular features of Jesus' earthly ministry, confirming signs that attested to the truth of His message and revealed who He was.

When evening had come, they brought to Him many who were demon-possessed. And He cast out the spirits with a word, and healed all who were sick, that it might be fulfilled which was spoken by Isaiah the prophet, saying: "He Himself took our infirmities and bore our sicknesses" (Matthew 8:16-17).

Jesus was doing just what Isaiah had described prophetically centuries earlier. Verse 17 says, "That it might be fulfilled which was spoken by Isaiah the prophet." This is why the Book of Isaiah is often referred to as "the gospel according to Isaiah." Jesus Himself "took our infirmities and bore our sicknesses." Simon Peter says just about the same thing:

"Who Himself bore our sins in His own body on the tree, that we, having died to sins, might live for righteousness—by whose stripes you were healed" (1 Peter 2:24).

Because our Passover Lamb went to Calvary, something awesome is happening that is shattering principalities and powers and setting free every family on earth. It happened 2,000 years ago and it is happening today, right now. Today we are being set free because Jesus, right now, is taking our sins and our sicknesses 2,000 years ago. How is this possible? Because He is the eternal Lamb of God. How this can be is one of God's great mysteries. How can He take our sins away? He is doing it right now, 2,000 years ago. This was an eternal moment. God did it, and right now we can connect and see our children healed. Right now we can connect and experience healing and deliverance from all oppression.

Jesus wore that crown of thorns so we could be set free. He endured the beatings and the flogging so we could be healed. He suffered the agony of those nails so our sins could be forgiven. He bore our sickness so He could give us perfect wholeness. When we plug into what Jesus did for us with His blood, we can see every curse broken.

Plug into what the Lord has done for you. Make the connection and make it personal: "Christ is redeeming *me*. He is redeeming *my* children. The devil has no jurisdiction over my kids. The curse is broken in my life and in my family." Exercise your faith. The more you release your faith in what Jesus did for you, the more His blood will avail for you and yours in everyday living.

D—Day and V-D Day

One of my favorite movies is *The Longest Day*, based on the book by Cornelius Ryan. It is an epic portrayal of the Allied invasion of Europe on June 6, 1944, a day known in history as D—Day. It was a day that changed history, a day that made the defeat of Nazi Germany inevitable. Although fighting continued for nearly a year after, the die was cast. Germany was doomed.

A lot was riding on the invasion. The Germans knew that if they could prevent the Allies from getting a foothold on the beaches, they could throw back the invasion and continue to control Europe. After Europe would come the world. For the Allies, failure to win the day on the beaches of Normandy would be a disastrous setback. It would take many months before another such attack could be attempted. The war would continue indefinitely, and many more lives would be lost.

Fortunately, the Allies prevailed. They established a foothold in France and from there began an advance that culminated almost a year later with the collapse and surrender of Germany in May of 1945. That day of victory became known as V-E-Day, Victory in Europe Day. Three months later, V-J-Day was born when Japan surrendered to the Allies. Had there not been D—Day, there would have been no V-E-Day. The invasion had to come in order to engage the enemy on his own territory, roll back his advances, and liberate the oppressed peoples of Europe.

D—Day determined V-Day. For us, Easter, or Resurrection Sunday, is V-Day, the day Jesus won the final victory over the enemy, satan. D—Day was the birth of Jesus, when the Son of God invaded the earth to fight satan on his own soil, turn back his advances, and liberate all the people he held in bondage.

The invasion has come. Victory is assured. For us, there is mainly just "mopping up" to do. It's all over for the powers of darkness. Evil has been forever defeated by the King of Glory, the Lamb of God. Because of D—Day 2,000 years ago, we have victory today. Jesus is the Passover Lamb who gave His life for our release. His blood was spilled, and satan was doomed. There is power in the blood of Jesus, wonder-working power. One drop of Jesus' blood is all it takes to destroy the kingdom of satan and all his works.

Hosanna in the Highest!

On His way to Jerusalem for the final time, Jesus stopped in the village of Bethany. This was about six days before His crucifixion. The next day, Sunday, He entered Jerusalem to great acclaim from the common people.

> *And a very great multitude spread their clothes on the road; others cut down branches from the trees and spread them on the road. Then the multitudes who went before and those who followed cried out, saying: "Hosanna to the Son of David! Blessed is He who comes in the name of the Lord! Hosanna in the highest!"* (Matthew 21:8-9).

For five days the people examined the Lamb and found Him perfect in every way. As Jesus entered the city, the people greeted Him with cries of "Hosanna!" This word is a direct transliteration from the Hebrew and literally means "Please save." It is a cry to God for help: "Save me!"

I remember when I was growing up in Africa, there was a man who "taught" swimming. Since there were no swimming pools where we were, we went out into the ocean to learn to swim. There was an old harbor where sharks were known to frequent. A swimming "lesson" consisted of having a rope tied around your waist and being thrown into the water. That's what happened to me. I had a rope tied around my waist, and I was thrown into the water.

Well, my body thinks it is made of iron, and it reacted to the water the way iron would. I went straight down. In my life I have had many near-death experiences. This was one of them. I came up gasping for air crying, "Save me, save me." The instructor ignored me. He simply said, "Swim, swim." I wasn't about to listen to him. He was holding onto the rope. I pulled on the rope. He fell into the ocean.

My desperate cry of "Save me, save me," catches the spirit of the original meaning of "hosanna." The people called out "Hosanna!" "Lord, please save!" That cry was followed immediately by "Blessed is He who comes in the name of the Lord!" They cried out and the Lord answered. They said, "Save me!" and He was there.

Gradually through the years, the word "hosanna" came to mean not just "save me," but "salvation" itself. The idea was that God responds so quickly to our cries to be saved that the cry for salvation and the act of salvation almost seem to become one. By the time the people of Jerusalem welcomed Jesus on that Palm Sunday, their cry of "Hosanna!" meant "Salvation is coming," or "Salvation is here." How right they were. God the Father sent salvation in the person of Jesus Christ, His Son.

Jesus was crucified on the 14th day of *Nisan*. There were probably a quarter of a million people in Jerusalem that week to celebrate Passover, so there could easily have been 150,000 to 200,000 people who cried "Hosanna," as Jesus entered the city. It was like the most anointed ticker-tape parade ever, better even than when the New York Yankees got a ticker-tape parade for winning the World Series, or when General Douglas

MacArthur came home. It was better than the parade for the rescued Apollo 13 astronauts, or the V-E-Day and V-J-Day celebrations.

It's Friday, but Sunday's Coming

Palm Sunday, 30 A.D., was the greatest parade in history. The King of Glory came to Jerusalem. Five days later, He offered Himself up completely as the Lamb of God whose blood took away the penalty of our sin. Paul wrote in Ephesians 2:13, "But now in Christ Jesus you who once were far off have been brought near by the blood of Christ." On the cross, Jesus took every sin, every curse, and every sickness upon Himself. As Isaiah prophesied and Matthew echoed, "by His stripes we are healed."

If you want to have an increase in the Spirit's anointing for your ministry, healing, and deliverance, connect with the Word of God. Fast over these Scriptures and others, and pray over them until they sink into your spirit and you become one with them. Until the Holy Spirit connects you with the Word of God, it just sits there. Lay hold of God's Word and make it yours.

The blood of Jesus given to redeem us from sin is the theme of the Bible. Most of us have no idea of the depth and magnitude of the power of the blood of Jesus. There is life in His blood. There is healing and wholeness in His blood. There is power in His blood to break every curse and release every captive.

On Friday, the 14th day of *Nisan*, 30 A.D., at 3:00 in the afternoon, the time of the slaying of the Passover lamb, Jesus died. It was a dark time. The Son of God was dead and buried. His followers scattered in shock and fear. It appeared as though evil had triumphed.

Appearances can be deceiving. God was not finished yet. As the old black preacher said, "It's Friday, but Sunday's coming!"

I don't care what you are going through today. Maybe the devil has attacked you physically, but don't worry. It's Friday, but Sunday's coming. He may be attacking your home or your marriage. Don't despair: It's Friday, but Sunday's coming. The devil may have stolen your health or your finances. Hang in there: It's Friday, but Sunday's coming. You may be discouraged, hurting, and depressed with dark shadows overwhelming you. Don't give up: It's Friday, but Sunday's coming.

Sunday brings resurrection, restoration, healing, and deliverance. Behold the risen King! Behold the Lamb of God who takes away the sin of the world! Behold the Lamb of God whose blood avails for you and your house! Behold the blood of Jesus, powerful enough to destroy satan's kingdom, break every bondage, and remove every curse! Behold the precious blood of Jesus Christ, our Passover Lamb, that gives us the victory!

For other books, audiotapes, or other resource material from the author, contact:

Mahesh Chavda Ministries International
P.O. Box 411008
Charlotte, NC 28241
(704) 543-7272
FAX: (704) 541-5300

E-mail: info@watchofthelord.com
www.watchofthelord.com

Books by Mahesh Chavda

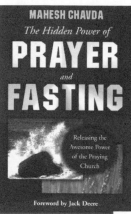

THE HIDDEN POWER OF PRAYER AND FASTING

The praying believer is the confident believer. But the fasting believer is the overcoming believer. This is the believer who changes the circumstances and the world around him. He is the one who experiences the supernatural power of the risen Lord in his everyday life. An international evangelist and the senior pastor of All Nations Church in Charlotte, North Carolina, Mahesh Chavda has seen firsthand the power of God released through a lifestyle of prayer and fasting. Here he shares from decades of personal experience and scriptural study principles and practical tips about fasting and praying. This book will inspire you to tap into God's power and change your life, your city, and your nation!
ISBN: 0-7684-2017-2

THE HIDDEN POWER OF THE BELIEVER'S TOUCH

Here is the fatal blow to the belief that God does not heal today. Through the power of his personal experience and the strength of his biblical insight. Mahesh Chavda reveals how the healing compassion of our Lord reaches the hurting masses simply by the believer's healing touch. Written with compassion, humor, and insight, *The Hidden Power of the Believer's Touch* affirms that the healing anointing and the gifts of signs and wonders are not reserved for "super saints" or the specially gifted, but are available to every believer who carries the compassion and love of the Lord Jesus.
ISBN: 0-7684-1974-3

THE HIDDEN POWER OF SPEAKING IN TONGUES

Almost 40 years ago John and Elizabeth Sherill introduced the world to the phenomenon of "speaking in tongues" in their book *They Speak With Other Tongues*. The book was an immediate success as thousands were touched by the power of this spiritual gift. *The Hidden Power of Speaking in Tongues* again explores this spiritual experience powerfully prevalent in the early Church. This much-maligned and controversial gift was a practical part of their worship and intercession and seeks to be rediscovered in our day. In a day of spiritual poverty, Chavda challenges the Body of Christ to experience afresh the secret dynamic of "speaking in tongues," as he removes the veil covering this glorious gift.
ISBN: 0-7684-2171-3

Available at your local Christian bookstore.

Additional copies of this book and other
book titles from DESTINY IMAGE are
available at your local bookstore.

For a bookstore near you, call 1-800-722-6774

Send a request for a catalog to:

Destiny Image® Publishers, Inc.
P.O. Box 310
Shippensburg, PA 17257-0310

*"Speaking to the Purposes of God for This
Generation and for the Generations to Come"*

**For a complete list of our titles,
visit us at www.destinyimage.com**